One American Woman
Fifty Italian Men

12-27-13

One American Woman Fifty Italian Men: A Journey of Cycling, Love, and Will

Published by Wheatmark®
1760 East River Road, Suite 145
Tucson, Arizona 85718 USA
www.wheatmark.com

Cover by Carolyn Grossman

ISBN: 978-1-60494-891-2 (paperback)
ISBN: 978-1-60494-900-1 (ebook)
LCCN: 2012950288

One American Woman
Fifty Italian Men

A Journey of Cycling, Love, and Will

LYNNE ASHDOWN

For my father, Frank Teasdel
and my sons, Eric Ashdown and Mark Ashdown

CONTENTS

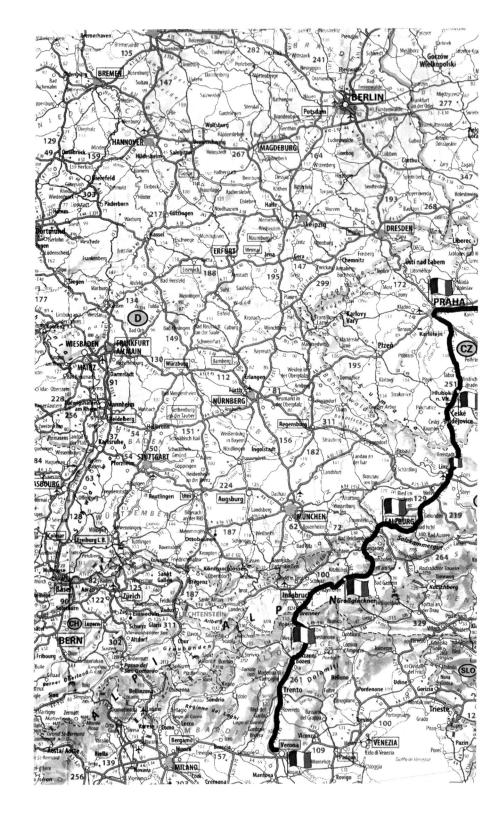

Approximation of cycling route:
Verona, Italy to Warsaw, Poland

1

THE JOURNEY BEGINS

In the Soup Now

The air was crisp in the early June morning, and it had an edge. The men milled about, cleats clicking on the ancient cobblestones, shouting greetings, shifting from one foot to the other, fussing with their bicycles, waiting for the start. The three vans carrying food, spare bicycles, and parts were buzzing with activity. One cyclist was on the roof of one of the vans affixing bicycles and wheels, while others helped and shouted instructions in their rapid-fire Italian, "*Attento le ruote!*" ("Watch the wheels!")

This would be the first cycling tour attempted into the formerly closed East since the borders had been opened this year, in 1990. We would be cycling almost a thousand miles from Verona, across northern Italy, Austria, Czechoslovakia, and Poland to Warsaw, in just ten days. I would be the only woman cycling with the fifty-four men.

Astride my bike, I rubbed my arms to take away the chill as the first rays of the sun sneaked into the little piazza. I glanced over at Nino, my partner for the trip and, I hoped, maybe for life, wishing I felt as calm as he looked. Reading my thoughts, he reached over and squeezed my shoulder. "*Corragio*, Lina. Don't worry, you'll be fine."

All of the men who would be cycling were here by now. Many looked to be around my own age, forty to fifty, some younger, some older. They were outrageously colorful in their club jerseys. One guy had a Chesini racing bike painted a red plaid, with a red jersey and cap to match. All of their exotically painted bicycles were sleek, expensive racing machines, and they all looked like experienced cyclists.

Nino, raised in the mountains of northern Italy until he immigrated to America in his twenties, conversed easily with the men in his native Italian. Feeling a little isolated, I turned my attention to the men. This was the first time I'd seen Italian cyclists in a group. I guess I'd been too nervous at the pre-trip meeting to notice what great-looking men they were, full of smiles, energy, and the joy of the moment. They had the same range of coloring as any group of Americans, yet there was something that set them apart; they were the most masculine group of guys I'd ever seen. They strutted and boomed in rich, low baritones, testosterone overflowing. Many of their wives and children were here to see us off, standing quietly by the edge of the piazza, somewhat awed by the goings-on.

This was a private trip, a combination of seven cycling clubs from the Verona region. It had been organized by a Dottore Germano Veronese, whom I had yet to meet. He seemed to be the force behind the trip, and general Big Cheese.

I'd hoped to sort of melt into the group, but it was not to be. By now everyone had heard that *una donna Americana* would be pedaling with the group. The men stared and pointed and were obviously discussing me. In other circumstances I loved attention, but now I wished I were ten pounds thinner, invisible, and preferably both. They examined my bicycle, my gears, my legs, and the rest of me. I wished I had the same confidence in myself that I had in my beautiful Italian bicycle. It was sort of like showing up in a Porsche when you'd just learned to drive. A wave of self-doubt washed over me, but I nodded, smiled, looked them in the eye, and tried not to look intimidated. Some of them smiled, shook hands, and introduced themselves, but the looks of a few said not everyone was thrilled I would be along. I couldn't understand a word being said. Feeling awkward and self-conscious, I nodded and smiled. I looked around for Nino, who had momentarily forgotten me and was chatting with someone across the piazza.

Antonio, who did all the hands-on organizing, rescued me. "Aaaah, Lina, Lina!" Antonio didn't speak English either, but he was such a friendly, loving, and outgoing man that I felt comfortable with him regardless of our language problems. Tall and sturdily built, he had a huge mustache, laughing brown eyes, and a deep, full voice with which he bellowed with great affection to his friends, who appeared to be everybody. I realized for the first time that due to my inability to speak with any of them, I was perceiving them on a nonverbal level—maybe a more accurate level of who they really were.

Antonio introduced me to Dottore, *il capo* (the boss). I knew it was certainly by his sanction that I'd been allowed to come. A highly respected medical doctor and a wealthy man, he'd been mayor of San Pietro in Cariano, which surrounded the little piazza where we were congregating. He was an influential political force here in the Verona region. Well over six feet and a big man from head to toe, he looked the part of Il Capo, moving about with the confident air of authority of someone who is used to being in charge. Antonio, his close friend, and everyone else addressed him as "Dottore." He looked more Germanic than Italian, with ruddy, fair skin and a shock of white hair. Although heavy, he looked very strong. His bulk told me this was a man who savored the finer things in life. His pale blue eyes, revealing the shrewd man behind them, appraised me as I shook his hand. But he greeted me warmly and made me feel he was glad to have me on the trip. A flood of relief washed over me, and I started to relax. Noticing that the cyclists were starting to mount up, I excused myself to find Nino. He'd been looking for me, to tell me a television crew was here to film the start of the trip. When they heard a woman would be cycling with the group, they wanted to interview me.

Just then someone stuck a microphone under my nose. I turned, startled, and found myself looking into a TV camera.

"We understand you are the first and only woman to cycle with an Italian men's touring group in Italy. How do you feel about that?"

Oh jeez. Without thinking, I proclaimed into the camera on national Italian television, "I am thrilled to be here, to be able to participate, and I hope to prove for all American women, and for all Italian women, that a woman can finish a trip like this on the bicycle and not in the van."

Omygawd! I'd announced the secret commitment I'd made to myself to the entire world. Shocked, I only just realized as I said it that I was doing this not just for myself but for other women, too.

Nino, who'd translated, rolled his eyes at the audacity of my statement. "Bless your heart, you're in the soup now," he said. He always said "Bless your heart" about someone who was about to do something stupid, impossible, or both.

Almost as surprised as he was, I looked at him and laughed, mostly at my own big mouth. Now I really had to do it.

The Italian Vacation

At home in California a few months before, a friend told me Nino had cycled across America, and that he was looking for a local cycling partner. Hey, what's to lose? Now in early middle age, I was just hitting my stride; I was up for adventure now more than ever. I'd called him, and we made a date to go for a hike.

I don't know what I expected when I opened the door, but I was immediately drawn to his rugged good looks, his tanned face and wavy white hair, his strong male energy. But for all his effusive greeting, there was something veiled about him; it struck me that this was a man who guarded his cards. I loved his vitality and was fascinated by what might lie hidden behind those unfathomable brown eyes, which hinted an intense intelligence. My characteristic American openness chose fascination with mystery over awareness of hidden agendas. In spite of the independent face I presented to the world, by the time he stepped inside the door my heart was asking: Could this be the guy I've been waiting for?

As we hiked the heavily wooded trails of Mt. Tamalpais near my home, Nino told me he'd attacked the sport of cycling for the first time only in his fifties. Now in his sixties, retired and widowed, he cycled regularly with the same vigor he used to run the twelve miles home from his brokerage office in downtown San Francisco.

We began cycling and dining together regularly. After our first dinner together at his place he'd whispered, "Please don't go."

I didn't. We savored every moment from then on, eating the delicious pasta he loved to fix, walking together in the evenings, discussing every subject under the sun. I loved hearing him talk about the art he wanted to show me in Italy—I loved hearing him talk about almost anything. And he loved talking to me, so engaged in life and so different from the women in his past. Soon we were fitting our lives around being together every day. I'd said yes immediately when he invited me to go to Italy with him in May.

One day during a coffee break on a bicycle ride, Nino mentioned in passing that he'd heard from a friend about a private cycling trip from Verona, Italy, to Warsaw, Poland, but he supposed it might be too much for us. Warsaw was, after all, only about a hundred miles from the Belarus border.

We were not serious cyclists; we just cycled for fun two or three times a week. "Oh sure, no problem," I'd joked, "and then we'll just cycle east to Moscow for dinner."

"Well, you never know," he said. "Why don't you bring your cycling gear, just in case?"

So I packed my gear. It might come in handy if we rented bikes somewhere. That was the last I thought of it as I became immersed in preparations for the trip and my growing relationship with Nino. Basking in each other's company, we spent hours planning our vacation in Italy. We shared an assumption that it would be the first of many in our future together. His veiled quality seemed to diminish as I grew comfortable in his company.

On the plane at last, I settled into my seat beside Nino, content in my complete trust in him. An experienced traveler, he knew his native Italy well. I looked forward to seeing *his* Italy. How wonderful it would be to relax and let someone else take the lead for a change. Mostly I'd traveled alone or as a single mother with my two boys, and I'd always been the one where the buck stopped. Luxuriating in the comfortable seat, I remembered the time in Tonga with the kids when I forgot the hotel vouchers; God, what a hassle *that* was. In retrospect, I guess I pictured myself being swept romantically and effortlessly along on Nino's capable arm through our little Italian adventure, savoring the possibility of a life together, sinking with blissful and intentional naïveté into the myth that someone else can direct your life, even if just for a little while.

Verona, Nino's favorite Italian city, would be our home base. As the train from Milan snaked lazily through the countryside, a patchwork collage of lush green fields and the red-tiled roofs and gardens of small, quiet towns filtered pleasantly into my consciousness.

I liked Verona immediately. Old, charming, and walkable, you could get a handle on it. The center of the city was dominated by a well-preserved Roman arena, home to a summer opera season. Adjacent to it was a grand central piazza, with elegant, small shops, restaurants, and narrow streets radiating out from it. It was a city that invited exploring on foot, rewarding us around corners with small piazzas surrounded by cafés and outdoor markets with bird sellers.

You could sit at one of the outdoor café tables set with a white tablecloth and silver table service, sipping a cappuccino, caressed by the mild, spring air, and lose yourself in the sensory overload of old, eternal Italy. There was something about the gleaming silver sugar and creamer and the act of stirring your cappuccino slowly with a silver spoon that bespoke a civilized, gracious life.

The next morning Nino said, "I think I'll give Dino a call; he's the contact for the bicycle trip."

Bicycle trip? Immersed in my new surroundings, I'd almost forgotten. Neither of us had met Dino; he was a friend of someone Nino knew at home. Nino called him and made a date for him to join us for dinner that night at our hotel.

The Invitation

Dino greeted us warmly. He was a tall, unassuming man, with thinning brown hair and blue eyes that smiled from a weather-hewn face. Lean and fit, he'd been a cyclist all his life. At dinner, he showed us the mileage and elevation maps for the trip to Warsaw. Though most of the conversation was in Italian, I realized for the first time that Nino was seriously interested in making the trip. I'd assumed that any trip here we'd do together, but suddenly I sensed that he was torn between the bicycle trip and me, as if they were separate agendas. The thought startled me, since I'd believed his new feelings for me were the most important reason for our trip here together. Then he asked Dino about the possibility of my going too; I could tell by the silence that settled over the table.

Dino could take the measure of a man. He leaned slightly toward me now, and stared into my eyes as if trying to measure my grit. I met his gaze. He knew he'd be in trouble with the men if I couldn't keep up. He asked Nino a question, indicating me with his head.

"What did he say?" I asked.

"He wants to know how many kilometers you have on your legs." Nino explained that cyclists here measure their conditioning by how many kilometers they've cycled since the beginning of the season, usually starting in March when the cold of the northern Italian winter begins to fade.

I asked him to tell Dino how much I cycled, which I knew was nothing to write home about. As a child I'd cycled regularly all over the Oakland hills until I discovered boys at the age of fourteen, but I didn't start cycling again as an adult until into my thirties. I was a little uneasy, unsure if what Nino was saying about me was accurate. For the first of many times to come, I felt completely exasperated by not understanding or speaking Italian. But even though I didn't understand the words, I understood that Dino was giving Nino a tentative okay if I wanted to go, too.

I looked at Nino, who hesitantly confirmed the invitation: "The route to Warsaw will be just under a thousand miles, to be covered in ten days." He added, over casually I thought, "Of course you know you'll be the only woman cyclist on the trip."

Of course I didn't know. My fork stopped mid-way to my mouth as I took in this splat to my consciousness. I knew women didn't cycle for sport in France, but I assumed women cycled in Italy, since Italy had produced Maria Canins, one of the world's greatest female bicycle racers. And I guess they do, somewhere. But I never did see a woman on a racing bicycle in Italy for sport. To the bakery, yes, but for sport, no. They even have special rear fenders on women's bicycles in Italy to prevent skirts from becoming caught in the spokes.

I looked at the two men, trying to figure out what was really going on. I was sure the only reason Dino had invited me was to get Nino to go. "If I'll be the only woman, why do you want me to go?" I addressed both of them.

Nino said, "I think you can do it, and it will be a great challenge." I looked at him hard. His handsome, distinguished face was inscrutable; he was a master at drawing a mask of impassivity over himself when he didn't want you to know what he was thinking. He was nobody's fool when it came to getting what he wanted. Did he mean it? I just didn't know. I did know that *he* wanted to go, and I didn't realize until this moment just how badly.

I turned to Dino. "Why do you want me to go?"

Nino translated his reply: "I talked to the organizers of the trip this afternoon, and they said it would be all right for you to try."

I raised an eyebrow; Nino hadn't mentioned that he and Dino had already discussed this. He said, "If you could do it, they think you'd be the first woman to travel on a bicycle with an Italian men's touring group. And you can always get in one of the vans if it gets too hard."

Aha. That was it. I'd end up in the van, then Nino could cycle with the men. *Oh, don't be so cynical,* I told myself. *Maybe they really do want you to go.*

Except for Dino, I hadn't met any of the cyclists yet, but I had a preconceived notion of what they would be like. Dino told me they'd range in age from the thirties to the sixties, and would have a wide range of cycling abilities. Still, I knew they'd probably all be stronger cyclists than I was. They'd be the stereotypical chauvinistic, macho Italian men, and I couldn't imagine their inviting me on such a trip. However, there it was; they had invited me.

We talked about the distances and the mountains. They'd average almost a hundred miles per day, some days more, some days less, for ten days. That in itself seemed almost impossible. Nino said, "Don't worry, we can ride at our own pace. We don't have to keep up with them."

I glanced at Dino. Since he couldn't understand English, I couldn't see his reaction to this remark. Nino continued, "Look, we can take all day to do it; it won't be as hard as it sounds." Later, I was to look back on these remarks as the first of the reasons I came to think of him as *Bum Dope Nino.* We looked at the elevation maps Dino had brought. There were a few bumps on the maps, such as the Brenner Pass at the Austrian border, which we'd cross on the second day. There were also a few hills in Austria, better known as the Alps, not to mention the Carpathian Mountains between Czechoslovakia and Poland. I kept silent for the rest of the dinner while they conversed in Italian, thinking about whether or not I was in touch with reality for even considering such a thing. Contrary to Nino's words, I had a gut feeling it would've been fine with him if I went along in the van with the wives who would come to help with the food, while he cycled with the men.

Married and divorced young, I'd raised my two sons alone and had done more than my share of cooking; passing out rolls at rest stops was not exactly what I had in mind for my Italian vacation. The thought of it made me angry, and I went to bed churning with indecision.

Our romantic vacation in Italy had changed completely. All either of us could think about now was the bicycle trip. Over breakfast the next morning, I asked him, "Do you really think I could do it?"

Nino buttered his roll with a studied nonchalance that told me he was sure *he* could do it, but not at all sure that I could. I began to be annoyed by his silence. He confirmed my suspicions. "On second thought, no, I don't think you can do it. I think you're in over your head. And they have a rule; no one may ride in the van unless his or her bike has broken down. So if you get in the van, you won't be able to ride again."

I drew back, shocked. This was not what I'd expected him to say. I knew I was almost as strong as he was, and inside, probably as strong as most men.

"And," he said, "you'd have to pay your own way, since I haven't budgeted for this."

My heart sank. He didn't want me to go. I knew he was conflicted; I thought the Italian part of him wanted to pedal with the men, but the American part of him wanted me to go, to show them all I could do it.

I decided not to discuss it with him further, but to think about it privately and make my own decision. The money wasn't a problem, but his attitude was. The trip was a couple of weeks off, so I said, "Let's go sightseeing and think about something else today."

We didn't think about something else that day. We walked around arm in arm, pretending to be in the moment with our relationship as we soaked up the ambience of Verona. But each of us was thinking our own private thoughts about the bicycle trip to Warsaw.

What if I could really do it? My heroine fantasies were kicking in. It wouldn't be a *we* thing, though, I realized. It would be an *I* thing. Was this what I really wanted? My thoughts churned. Although a lifelong athlete, which nobody here knew except me, I hadn't really trained for a sport in many years, since the five mile swims I'd ploughed through as a teenager or the course after course I'd run learning the slalom. Common knowledge in youth-oriented American culture had you heading downhill after fifty. But Dino had said that many of the men cycling would be around that age, and Nino was in his sixties. I was fifty-two. Why couldn't I do it if they could do it?

By the end of the day I realized I wanted desperately to go on this trip, wanted to be a real cyclist, to stretch the limits of what I could do. I couldn't see it yet, but I felt it, knew it was there: this some-thing—this cyclist—I could become. It had taken me over.

2

Paradigm Shift

The Deal

After we returned to the hotel, Nino took a nap. While he slept, I spread out the maps of Austria and eastern Europe we'd just bought and studied the elevations on the route we'd take. It didn't look too bad, since we were used to cycling hills at home. Of course, the maps didn't indicate the steepness of the climbs, but you could still get a rough idea of the grades by gauging the distance and change of elevations. The first big climb looked pretty formidable: the Brenner Pass into Austria. It was a four-thousand-foot climb, most of which we'd do on the second day. Dino had talked about this, and he'd said there was only one really steep section of the climb, for three kilometers. *Hey*, I thought, *I can walk parts of it if I have to; I can do anything for three kilometers, a little less than two miles.*

During a summer in France the previous year, I'd taken my bicycle on a last-minute whim. Cycling almost every day, I'd done some loop rides that had taken more than all day. Occasionally finding myself with fifteen miles to go when it got dark, I learned that you still have to pedal home even if you've completely run out of food, water, strength, and daylight. For endurance and sheer force of will, cycling was in a class by itself and certainly the most demanding sport I'd ever tried.

I'd done a few hundred-mile rides—but none back-to-back, let alone ten. Was cycling on this trip a reasonable goal for me? Rationally it didn't seem so. I tried to see into the fiber of my being, tried to see the extent of my own strength. But even as I turned this over and over in my mind, I knew. My gut said I could do it.

Why was this becoming so all-consuming and important? I don't have to prove myself to anybody! But I did. As a young single mother after a divorce, I'd put to work my early dream of becoming a professional singer. Singing at night in local clubs, I'd struggled to provide enough money for us, and I'd hated having to ask my disapproving mother for help. The time came for me to go on tour. I gave it up because of my commitment to being a parent, to being present for my kids. I quit before I was ready to quit. Now I desperately needed to own my power, to bring to completion what I said I'd do—to show my mother, who always said I'd never make it without her; to show my father, who always believed I could; and most of all to show *me* I could stand up in the world and do what I said I would do.

It struck me how little Nino really knew me. But then I'd camouflaged the part of myself that had been honed by life's hard choices and by my years of training for sports. Nino's attitude—she's just a woman; she'll never make it and it's not important anyway; she'll probably be relieved and just as happy to be passing out rolls with the other wives—brought all of the unfinished agendas of my life roaring to the surface, baring naked and raw my past insecurities about who I was, what I could do, and the strength and resolve of my will. My dilettante days were over.

So I made a deal with myself in the mirror. If I go, I will finish the trip on the bicycle. It won't matter how poorly I do it, just that I do it—that I finish—on the bicycle. Quitting will not be an option. I'll try not to let it matter how I look to the men. Just that I finish. For me. For my father. Could I live with that?

Yes.

Deal.

The Bicycle

When I told Nino of my decision, he said he was glad I'd decided to go, but I sensed that he was less than thrilled. I didn't understand this new duality I'd uncovered in him, so I decided to ignore it. Maybe I was seeing dragons where there were none.

Dino had already reserved bicycles for us to rent at Carpentieri's, his favorite bike shop in Riva, at Lake Garda. But how could Dino know what I wanted or needed?

A funny thing happens to a woman sometimes when she is with a man. Even the most independent woman, one who has raised her family and managed a career alone, can give up her independence. There is no conscious decision made about it. It's an insidious thing. Suddenly you find yourself following him around, asking him questions to which you already know the answer, letting him lead you around by the elbow as if you were a helpless blob. It's seductive, and you can succumb to it.

I'd become conscious of this phenomenon years before, watching myself slip into it during other times in my life. It was a giving up of one's own power. Was it gender genetics? Influence of a collective unconscious? A search for approval from men seeking ego support rather than the companionship of an equal? Childhood behavior modification from my mother? I've never known.

But here in Italy with Nino, I'd been enjoying this being led around by the elbow, this vacation from responsibility. But as the trip took on the reality of acquiring a bicycle, I knew I'd have to switch back into my independent gear to insist on the right bicycle: a light, high-quality one with low gears that would help me make it to Warsaw. This might entail some assertive behavior, of which I also had a repertoire. Nino hadn't seen that side of me yet.

During the drive with Dino to the bicycle shop, from the backseat I thought about having to be two different women now: the agreeable, glamorous woman who is an Italian man's traveling companion, and a cyclist tough enough to cycle with fifty men across four countries to Warsaw. The magnitude of what I was about to attempt was seeping fully into my awareness. As the only woman on the trip, it was even more significant that I would be the first woman to do such a trip in Italy. I'd always worked hard at keeping my naïveté, my belief in life's possibilities, and I worked hard at it now. I forced myself to focus on the scenery outside the car window.

Dino was taking a detour to show us the first part of the route we'd be pedaling. We'd head north up Highway 12, which roughly paralleled the autostrada toward the Brenner Pass. At the summit was the Austrian border. Highway 12, a lightly traveled two-lane road, wended its way through the *Val* (valley) *d'Adige*, alongside the Adige River. The route appeared almost flat, but rose imperceptibly to what appeared to be a wall at the end of the long valley. *Oh my God*, I thought, *how will I get over that?* But as we continued north I could see a pass through the wall, and it looked less impossible.

Dino explained that we'd be expected to average about twenty-eight kilometers, or seventeen miles, per hour. He said the food and rest stops were predicated on that pace. Ah. Now I understood. Of course we wouldn't be able to keep our own pace. We'd have to get to where the food would be, with the rest of them. Food for a cyclist is like gas for a car. No gas, no food, no engine. We'd have to keep up.

As the rolling vineyards and sleepy country villages flashed by the car window, I couldn't get the trip out of my mind. I must succeed. Not to do so would be unthinkable. *I will ride all the way if it takes twelve hours a day*, I thought. My father, long since passed but still with me in spirit, and Angelo, my guardian angel whom I discovered sitting on my left shoulder while cycling last year in France, will help me. But what if I couldn't make it? What if I failed in front of all those men? How could I live with it? To them I'd be just a woman, but to me I'd be one of them. I closed my eyes, said a silent prayer, and tried to relax and let it go.

I walked into the bicycle shop with a chip on my shoulder that I hoped didn't show, sure that Nino would be given a good bike and I would be given some clunky monster. My hand tightened around the not-so-thick wad of traveler's checks in my purse. I hadn't mentioned it to Nino, but I was prepared to spend all of it and use my credit card to buy a good bicycle, if that's what it took. Nino had no idea of the depth of my commitment.

The owner, Carpentieri, all smiles and Italian good cheer, greeted Dino warmly. We were introduced; he knew who we were and why we had come. He, Nino, and Dino chatted for awhile. I looked around, unable to participate in the Italian conversation. With me trailing at the rear, Carpentieri led us downstairs to get the bicycles he'd picked out. For Nino, he had a snappy Colnago racing bike. The fit was perfect, Nino was thrilled, and there was much conversation about it.

Finally I cleared my throat. Oh yes, the woman—they remembered I was there. *Una bicicletta per la donna!* Let's see what we can do. I could see this was the first time Carpentieri had considered the issue. He looked me over and pointed to a stock ten-speed on a rack with upright handlebars. My worst fears were confirmed. I told Nino, "Please tell him that you and I will be pedaling on the same trip." Nino did, and there was a long silence. Dino had told him previously, but he must not have heard it.

Carpentieri immediately eyeballed my legs, doing his own reality check. "Are you sure you can do this?" he asked, in Italian.

I paused. "No, but I'm going to do it, or I'm going to die on the bicycle," I said, looking at him levelly, not smiling. His face changed as Nino translated. More silence. I asked Nino how to say "need" and "good," and stammered my first sentence in Italian. "I need a good bicycle—*Bisogna buon bicicletta.*"

The mood shifted, and I could see now that Carpentieri wanted to help me. He walked around, looking at me, looking at the bikes on the racks. He took down a sleek red and white racing bike and brought it over. I still thought it would be a lousy bike, but it said "Moser" on the frame, and I figured this Italian bicycle racing legend wouldn't put his name on a lousy bike. It was very light, and the more I looked at it the better it looked. I asked if I could try it out.

A commotion of chivalry ensued when I tried to carry the bike up the stairs, like I do at home. I laughed as they argued good-naturedly over who would carry the bike up. Never mind that I would pedal it across eastern Europe; I'd take my chivalry wherever I could get it. Carpentieri ceremoniously handed the bike over to me at the door, and they all stood and watched as I rode the bike up and down the street.

It was the same thrill you'd get riding a great horse for the first time. Quick, light, and steady, this was a wonderful bike! If any bike could get me to Warsaw, this one could. I gave them the thumb- up as I pedaled by, and they gave it back to me. It was great to be back on the bike, to be alive! I was ashamed of my earlier, sullen attitude, seeing the lengths they'd gone to help me and that they genuinely wished me well. I vowed to have only positive expectations from now on.

Carpentieri fitted the bike with a different saddle, toe clips, water bottle, pump, and pack. He installed a smaller sprocket for a climbing gear in the back. The chain rings in front were no match for the low "granny gear" I had on my bike at home (a third chain ring providing low gears for climbing added to the two front chain rings—the equivalent of adding four-wheel drive to the family car). I thought—hoped—it would do.

3

TRAINING

The Test

Nino and I would ride the new bikes back to our hotel, and Dino would stay a little ahead in his car to show us the way. He told us to try to maintain sixteen miles per hour, the minimum pace planned for the trip.

Soon we were out of the traffic of Riva and pedaling south on the east shore of the magnificent Lake Garda. It was a deep blue, with mountains rising directly out of the lake on the opposite side. In the quiet of the late afternoon, an ethereal mist hung over the lake. We pedaled south past elaborate villas and small hotels, gardens over-flowing with flowers, past windsurfers and people sunbathing on the shores of the lake.

Dino came into view ahead, leaning on the back of his car. He was concentrating on something in his hand. What was he doing? Oh my God, a stopwatch. He's timing us. So that's what this is about; he wants to see if we can really cut the mustard. When we caught up with him he told Nino, "Step it up to see if you can keep a faster pace."

We did, to faster than I'd ever cycled at a steady pace. The traffic and rough edge of the pavement forced me to keep my eyes on the road. The landscape flew by; I was missing most of it. I hoped we'd come back here in a car sometime, so I could look at the scenery. Suppressing my slight dismay, I wondered how I could keep up this pace. Would they really cycle this fast on the trip? Nino, who had a cyclometer on his bike, shouted back that we were going twenty-two miles per hour. Well, I noted privately, we have a tailwind and I do not really share his faith that we'll be able to keep this up. I made a note to get a cyclometer for my own bike, so I could monitor speed and distance for myself.

I was tempted to draft him, but I'd noticed since we'd been riding together that sometimes he rode erratically, or perhaps he just didn't think about the person cycling so close behind him. Frequently he'd hit his brakes without warning for a pothole, or because he wanted to look at something. I didn't feel safe staying any closer than about three feet from his back wheel—not close enough to get much drafting benefit.

Drafting—following inches behind another rider's back wheel to get the benefit of being in the slipstream—makes pedaling about twenty percent easier and helps conserve strength and energy on long rides. It requires skill and constant mindfulness from both the leader and the follower. I really didn't know how to do it, and confident proclamations to the contrary, neither did Nino.

Dino stopped to time us every ten kilometers. Finally we turned away from the lake and headed back east toward Verona. At least Dino was smiling his approval now, as he turned off toward his own home. As we waved good-bye I hoped I was smiling bravely. Actually, I was feeling pretty good. We'd covered forty-five miles in three hours, including a few short climbs. I had no idea I could do that.

At the hotel, we made macho jokes about the ride as we dressed for dinner. "I'm really surprised you could do that," Nino said. As he spoke of his concern for me, I knew that he was also worried about being able to do the trip himself, about what he'd gotten both of us into. Were both of us letting macho dreams of glory get in the way of reality? As for me, the pioneer spirit of my ancestors who had crossed the country in wagon trains was activated into full swing, and it was too late to turn it off. As for Nino, beneath his distinguished and conservative exterior lay the toughest of Italian men. He hadn't been a member of the *Alpini* (the Italian mountain troops) who fought the Russians in World War II for nothing.

Nino

Dino would go with us on a training ride today, in the afternoon. With the morning free, we decided to explore the village center of San Pietro in Cariano, the suburb of Verona where our hotel was located. This was the Valpolicella region, the wine country of northern Italy. The towns in this region are surrounded by rolling vineyards and green hills, often topped by a castle or a chateau at the end of a lane lined with tall, stately junipers. An unusual feature of the country-side was that farms, light industry, modest homes, and huge chateaux were mixed together in a delightful, laid-back, spread-out mix of Italian semirural life.

San Pietro, at first glance, appeared to be a present-day suburb surrounded by spacious homes and gardens, with a supermarket, a café, and a few stylish shops close to our modern hotel.

But a short walk up a hill revealed a different San Pietro. A small stone piazza was surrounded by buildings hundreds of years old, now occupied by small shops. The morning sun warmed the yellowed, earth-hued stone of the old walls. A great shade tree graced the center of the piazza, spreading its boughs magnanimously over most of the piazza. People were going quietly about their business, exchanging morning greetings. An old fountain, its sculptured shapes worn round with age, occupied one end of the piazza. Part of the fountain was a monument to the World War I and World War II dead. We read the names sadly, noting how much longer was the list for World War I. Europe's population had been decimated by World War I, and by World War II the villages had fewer young men to give. But war statistics don't have the same impact as reading the names of a village's own fallen sons, brothers, and husbands.

On the way back to the hotel, we came upon a monument to the Julia Regiment of the Alpini, Italy's great heroes of World War II, of which Nino's Monte Cervino battalion had been a part. Born and raised in northern Italy, Nino had been a young Alpini recruit at the beginning of the war. The Alpini were and are the elite Italian mountain troops, most of whom, like Nino, were skilled skiers and climbers from the mountain villages of northern Italy.

At that time Mussolini wanted to retain control over Italy's African colony, Ethiopia, despite the opposition of the League of Nations. He made a deal with Hitler. Mussolini would send a battalion of men to Russia to fight with the Germans against the Russians if Hitler would support Italy's efforts in the civil war in Ethiopia. So Mussolini sent 1,050 of Italy's best young men to fight alongside the Germans, knowing they'd have little chance against the Russians during a Russian winter. Nino was one of the few who survived.

Nino never would have left Italy after the war, except for marrying an American girl who had come to Italy to visit her relatives. He'd been struck by the thunderbolt of love, even though he spoke no English and she no Italian. After an exuberant Italian village wedding, they'd come to America. He was twenty-seven. With his new American wife, he arrived in San Francisco with the confidence of a man tested by war. With this experience, a university education, and a photographic memory, he had an instinctive bent for what works in the world.

With no money, family help, or knowledge of the language, he landed his first job as a night janitor at the Tosca Café in San Francisco's Italian North Beach neighborhood. The Pacific Stock Exchange was nearby. Soon he was learning English and successfully playing the market with their small savings, to the despair of his young wife. He captured the interest of a brokerage house, where he enjoyed a long and successful career as a broker. He passionately loved his new country and its ideals of freedom, and proudly became an American citizen. He and his wife raised two sons, and eventually he was widowed.

Nino's marriage had been a comfortable one. It had been an old-style Italian marriage; she had acquiesced to his judgment, and that had been that. He'd never been emotionally challenged by a woman—a wall I'd butt my own hard head against later.

But Italy remained Nino's great love. Since he retired, he'd returned there every summer. I watched him become a different person when he was in Italy, when he spoke Italian. The first time I'd seen this was soon after we met, in a North Beach Italian bookstore in San Francisco, where by chance we ran into an old Italian friend of his. I was accustomed to Nino's distinguished and reserved demeanor. But when he started to speak Italian, his whole face lit up in smiles, his arms and hands became suddenly animated, he talked a blue streak, and I felt faced with a whole other person.

This now very Italian Nino whooped for joy when he spotted the monument to his Alpini battalion. I was happy to be with a man with such a courageous history.

The Training Ride

Dino arrived at the hotel on his bicycle after lunch. "We'll ride through some beautiful country today," he told us, "but this will be a training ride."

Dino had been a life-long bicycle racer. His body was lean and hard, all muscle and sinew. His shoulders were slightly crooked, betraying more than a few old cycling injuries and making him look like the old war-horse of a cyclist that he was. He was a retired stone-cutter, and cycling was his life.

We set off. The air was redolent with things one savors: hints of freshly baked bread, a fine marinara, coffee, green things growing.

He must be kidding with this pace. Silently, I gave thanks when we had to slow down at intersections. No time to think; I was too busy keeping an eye on traffic and keeping up to even grasp my water bottle.

Soon we were out in the country on long, flat stretches of road, and I became more accustomed to the faster pace. Pulling in my elbows and stretching out forward and low over the handlebars to copy Dino's aerodynamic position on the bike, I noticed my resistance to the wind was reduced, and my speed increased.

I began to experiment with my gears, getting acquainted with the new bicycle. Riding this fast required a different pattern of shifting than I was accustomed to. Dino dropped back to see what I was doing. *Ah, that's it,* I thought, finding the right gear. He speeded up again, motioning with his head to follow him. *God, I can't pedal that fast and hard, dammit, I just can't do it!*

Yes, I can. Something shifts in the doing of it, and I can. I was pedaling fast and steady now, keeping up and keeping it up longer than I ever thought possible.

Sometimes Nino would get in front of me to pull. I'd pretend to draft, but would always stay at least three feet back. Why didn't I want to accept help from him? I didn't fully understand why I didn't like following so close behind him on the bicycle; there was more to it than the issue of drafting. My heart wasn't sure if his offers of help were sincere or without condescension. Observing that he thought only of himself when he rode, I shunned implications for the future and tried to think of other things. Meanwhile I rode a safe three feet behind his wheel.

Nino and Dino became engrossed in conversation, so I dropped back a little. With my legs spinning on the pedals and my body operating like the machine I knew it was supposed to be, I could relax and look around a little. The warmth of the sun crept through my shirt, warming my back. I basked in the quality of the light, so different from California. The sun was filtered through an ever-present haze, softening everything, like in Cezanne's paintings. Farm and village buildings were of earth hues, in shades of peach. The rolling hills were an inviting muted green, interlaced with vineyards.

I put my hands on the handlebar drops to maximize my speed. The speed thrilled me; I could do this forever! My bicycle and I became part of the road, part of the land that flashed by. It was the same feeling of being totally alive that I used to get skiing downhill as fast as I could.

Eventually I began to tire, wondering if we'd ever stop to rest. We didn't. Nino and Dino dropped back, and Nino translated for Dino that I must learn to draft to keep up. I tried, but eventually they pulled away from me. Dino dropped back again, telling Nino to tell me again that I must learn to keep up with the pack by drafting. *He's noticed I won't get any closer to Nino's wheel than three feet.* I couldn't tell him why, since I didn't speak Italian and didn't want to criticize Nino.

Dino continued instructing me how to draft, with Nino translating. "Even if the rider in front is going faster than you can go drafting, you must grit your teeth, endure the pain and keep drafting. He'll tire in a hundred yards or so himself because he won't be able to keep up his sprint while he's trying to shake you off," he instructed me, as if I were a junior racer. "Copy his gear to spin at exactly the same rate as he does. If you spin faster or slower, he'll be able to drop you." Dino, pedaling beside me, signaled me to drop down a gear so I could spin faster, like he did. Then he signaled me to get in back of him to draft. I noticed he was very smooth, and I knew he was aware of my presence on his wheel every minute. He motioned to come closer, and I ventured within six inches or so of his rear wheel. Now I could really feel being in the slipstream, and my pedaling became noticeably easier.

One of my heroine fantasies popped into my head. I saw myself drafting the men on the trip, with them trying to shake me off like a pesky fly, and me hanging on for dear life, gaining their respect.

We rode like this for a long time. A castle flew by out of the corner of my eye, but I didn't dare look at it, didn't dare take my eyes off Dino's wheel. I felt a flash of regret at missing all the sights, but I was so grateful to experience the thrill of the speed produced by my legs and this wonderful machine that the regret quickly passed. There was nothing I'd rather be doing than what I was doing right this second: following Dino, flying down the road faster than I ever thought I could.

I slowed on the hills, missing my granny gear, but at least I was steady. Dino told Nino he was very impressed with how fast and consistent I was on the flat, but I must learn to spin faster in a higher gear, and draft if it killed me, to stay with the pack. I was pleased and flattered he'd taken enough interest to teach me.

We kept up the pace all the way back to the hotel, riding in silence. Nino and I exchanged eye-rolling glances from time to time. Watching him pedal, I thought, *He's more than half a generation older than I am; if he can do it, I can do it.* Pain and fatigue finally overtook our enthusiasm, and we were both grateful to see San Pietro ahead, and our hotel. We waved good-bye to Dino, who had to pedal another twelve miles home, and who looked fresh as a daisy.

We stashed our bikes in the hotel basement, and made our way shakily to our room.

"Tell me you're not tired!" I demanded.

"Of course not. How could I be tired?" He waved his hands wildly, forgetting for a moment that when he was speaking English he wasn't supposed to do that. "Of course I'm tired! What do you think, that I have four balls? I gave two to you today, for crissakes!"

I rolled on the bed with laughter, almost falling on the floor. "I'll just borrow them for the duration of the trip," I joked.

We tried to walk normally down to dinner, having agreed not to discuss our tired legs or the hundred-mile training ride around Lake Garda tomorrow with Dino. We easily turned all our attention toward our meal, since nobody in the world makes pasta like the

Italians. After a huge dinner of tortellini l'orange, veal, and spinach with butter, cheese, and garlic, we fell exhausted into bed, too tired to think of anything but sleep.

At least I was.

4

TERROR IN THE TUNNELS DAY

Of Course It's Safe, or Why Are We Going?

Dino's son, Guido, joined us the next day for the ride around Lake Garda. I was surprised to discover he spoke English, the first I'd heard since arriving in Italy. Guido was pleasant and outgoing, and I looked forward to visiting with him on the ride. He was in his thirties, a successful businessman with a wife and new baby. Like his father, he'd been a bicycle racer for much of his life. Guido seemed open and supportive. I decided to seek all the cycling instruction from him that he was willing to give.

They arrived at the hotel to pick us up at seven thirty. Again the pace was too fast, but I was saved by stoplights until we were out in the country. Now we could ride side by side, and I peppered Guido with questions.

"What do you think of my position on the bike? Should I ride with my hands on the brake hoods or on the handlebars? Do I drop my heels too far when I'm pedaling? How about the way I use the gears? How fast should I spin? How do you spin the pedals so fast? It seems impossible!"

I told myself not to become discouraged; they were all stronger than I was and could therefore go faster. Everything they did was twice as hard for me when I did it at their speed. But whatever the odds, taking part in the upcoming trip had become an all-consuming goal. At that moment, my only reason for being was to be able to complete this trip on my bicycle.

Even though they were stronger, I was beginning to see that if I concentrated on my skills in drafting, I'd have a good chance of keeping up with them in the flat. I'd fall behind in the hills no matter what, but being able to keep up on the flat would at least make it feasible for me to go with them. And maybe they wouldn't all be stronger than I was. Maybe.

When we rode in congested areas, Guido dropped back and rode two feet out in the road to protect me from traffic. I wasn't used to this chivalry on the bicycle. Dino rode in the front, and Nino was in the rear. We didn't talk much. Today I noticed more of my surroundings, becoming more accustomed to the faster pace and the sustained effort.

Every five miles or so we'd pedal through a village. People were out hoeing the lettuce in their gardens, visiting with a neighbor over a fence. The pace of life was leisurely, and there always seemed to be time to visit with a friend in a café. Life felt manageable in Italy, and I felt very much at home.

There were other cyclists on the roads, all men, alone or in small groups. They were good riders on expensive racing bikes, dressed to the teeth in brilliant color-coordinated shorts, jerseys, and cycling caps. Only a few wore helmets. Soccer may be the sport to watch in Italy, but cycling is the sport to do.

We stopped for a quick coffee at a bar-café. Four other cyclists were there, one attracting all the attention. He was tall, lean, and handsome, and talked the most and loudest. He seemed to swagger even when he was sitting down. He draped his six-foot-plus frame over a chair beside his expensive racing Kestrel, in such a way as to show off a very recent road rash that covered much of one side of his body. It was barely starting to heal. No helmet, no bandages, more guts than brains—so this was macho, Italian style.

Over the last hill, the deep blue of Lake Garda filled the view almost as far as the eye could see both to the north and south. Stark, bare mountains rose almost vertically out of the other side of the lake. Straining to see the road on the other side, I couldn't make it out; it seemed as if the mountains rose straight up from the lake.

We turned south, and started our clockwise ride around the lake. We cycled past stately villas and resorts on the lakeshore. Were there any poor people in northern Italy? Certainly not on the shores of Lake Garda. It was still early, and everything was quiet.

At ten thirty they stopped for a brief rest. I was trailing behind a little, and by the time I arrived they'd finished their bananas. Everybody stood on one foot and then the other while I ate mine. I resisted the urge to swallow it in large chunks. Time to go; two and a half minutes had been their idea of a rest stop. Well, okay. Guido told me we had a long way to go, and asked if we'd brought our flashlights.

Flashlights? I glanced at Nino. He remembered they'd mentioned it, but he'd forgotten. Whatever for? Dino explained it to Nino in Italian, and Guido, looking worried, told me about the tunnels on the other side of the lake.

"There are no lights in the tunnels, and they are very long and dangerous," he said. "There are a whole series of them. Some are so dark that you can't see light at either end of the tunnel, and it can happen that you don't know which side of the road you're on." I was listening, but not wanting to hear this. "If this should happen to you," he continued, "you should stop immediately until you get your bearings." I refused to believe they could be that bad, or why were we going there? Trusting them, I'd put myself in their hands. "If a bus comes," Guido went on, "I will yell at you to stop. Stop immediately, get off your bike, pull it in close, and spread-eagle yourself against the wall of the tunnel." Oh my God. Dino had a small flashlight hanging from a string around his neck. Was he kidding, or what? I glanced from one to the other. Nobody was kidding. Nino and I looked at each other, but what was there to say? Nino didn't seem worried. But I was worried. What did they think we'd do with a flashlight, hold it in our teeth? They'd probably said, "bike light," but Nino had translated, "flashlight." Well, it was too late now.

Dino would lead the way, with the swinging, string-around-the-neck-special. "Dino forgot his regular prescription glasses," Nino told me. "I hope this won't be a problem when he takes off his sunglasses in the tunnels." I decided not to register this thought. They instructed me to stay behind Dino, and Guido would be right behind me. Nino would bring up the rear, in total darkness.

We pedaled a while longer in silence, and I could see we were turning north now, toward the tunnels. We stopped just before entering the first tunnel. Nino, apparently not having listened to all the instructions, cycled on ahead. Guido startled me by shouting a command for him to stop. The approach to the first tunnel was supported by columns that let in light and enabled us to see Nino waiting for us ahead at the entrance to the first tunnel.

We entered the tunnel single file. A shock of cold air rushed out and hit me in the face as the dark enveloped us. Dino's light barely illuminated the curb inside the tunnel, which Guido had also warned me about. The tunnel was carved out of the rock of the mountain, and water dripped from above. The sound of my tires told me the pavement was wet, but I couldn't see it. I knew how easy it would be to lose my equilibrium here in the dark, because this had happened to me more than once cycling home in the dark last year in France. There was no light now, and the bouncing, weak beam from Dino's flashlight was starting to make me dizzy. I fought it off, steadying myself by concentrating on the faint outlines of Dino's back, shadowed in the beam of his light. As we rode on, my heart pounded even as I denied the danger to keep myself calm.

Suddenly Guido shouted in alarm to Dino in Italian and then to me in English, telling me to stop and hug the wall because a bus was coming.

I braked to a halt, feeling my tires slip a little on the wet pavement. The sound of the big diesel engine coming toward us pumped adrenalin into my veins. I fumbled out of my toe clips and pressed my back against the wall, hugging my bike tight against me. Danger drilled through every pore of my body and the cold and wet of the tunnel wall seeped through my shirt as the bus roared past. It felt about a foot away.

"Nino, are you there? Are you all right?" I yelled, my voice echoing in the dark. He answered that everything was fine. I wished he'd asked if everything was all right with me, which it wasn't. Shaking, I felt my way back into my toe clips, wondering why I'd trusted these men so blindly.

Now we were out of the first tunnel. No sooner had I heaved a sigh of relief and lifted my head to the sun than we were into the next one.

Guido yelled something to Dino, real fear now in his voice. Cars came at us. The headlights blinded me, and I drifted over the center line. Guido yelled to get back over to the right. I did, but I couldn't gauge how far I was from the curb against the tunnel wall, invisible in the dark. It was a toss-up which was worse: the blinding headlights or the complete darkness.

Motorcycles came up behind us then, and slowed behind us so we'd have the benefit of their headlights. Once out of the tunnel, they passed.

Into the next one, and the next. Some were short, some long and completely dark. The short distances between them only served to blind us as we entered the next one. In a few, cars followed us slowly, illuminating our way with their headlights, like the motorcycles had done. Out of the tunnel, they passed us. Just as I began to feel safe, a group of motorcycles passed us too close in the next dark tunnel at unbelievably high speeds, the whine of their engines filling me with terror, affecting my balance. *Don't waver! Breathe! God, please don't let me fall. Will this never end?*

Then in still another long, dark stretch, Dino began to wobble. He slowed and almost fell, having trouble keeping his balance. *Oh God, the glasses problem. Please ride steady.* But he didn't. Guido shouted at him to move over and then shouted at me to pass him and go ahead.

Riding past him, now without the benefit of even Dino's dim, swinging light, I pulled the center line into my vision from an almost invisible black field, concentrating on pedaling steadily just to the right of it. I was afraid to move farther to the right because I couldn't see where the curb was. I had no idea where the others were, and I didn't dare risk my balance by turning my head. It was just me and the dark island of my bicycle.

Eventually it was over, and they caught up with me outside the last of the tunnels at the north end of the lake. Had there been twelve? Fifty? I hadn't counted. Now I realized why I hadn't been able to see the road from the other side of the lake: it was mostly inside the mountain! Guido explained that when Dino took off his prescription dark glasses he couldn't see very well, and tended to get dizzy in the tunnels. *Swell*, I thought. *What if we'd fallen like a house of cards and cars had come?* A surge of anger went through me, and I was glad my glasses hid most of my face. Why had they taken us through these tunnels? It had been way beyond the margin of acceptable risk, in my book.

Would there be tunnels like this on the trip? I hoped not. But at least we'd be with a group, and there would be safety in numbers. Had they taken us here to see how we'd handle it? How I'd handle it? Probably.

Now we were passing through a resort area with huge, grand old hotels and lakeshore communities heavily populated with German tourists. Suddenly the whole episode seemed like a bad dream, as if it had never happened. We continued to barrel along, keeping an uncomfortably fast pace.

Finally we arrived at Riva di Garda, the town where we had rented the bikes. At last they decided to stop for lunch. Nino heard Dino say to Guido, "Well, she passed the test—a fast one hundred kilometers." Ha. I knew it. We ordered our food, and Guido explained that there were no lights in the tunnels because the environmentalists lobbied to keep them dark in order to protect the bats.

"Great," I said. "Save a bat, kill a cyclist." Too drained and angry to expostulate further, I focused on the prospect of the pizza, although I could've used a steak, some garlic mashed potatoes, a little merlot, and a ride home.

Guido and Dino went on alone to finish their fast ride, leaving Nino and me to finish our lunch and ride home at a more leisurely pace. The big ride was a week off. We were as ready as we were going to be able to get, and planned to ride easy and rest until the start of the ride. After acquiring a cyclometer for my bike at Carpentieri's, we headed home.

During the leisurely ride back to our hotel, admiring the daisies beside the road, I thought about the fear I'd felt in the tunnels. When the little things scare you, you can indulge the fear, get angry, or react any way you choose. But when you find yourself in a situation like this one, you're too damn busy trying to get yourself out of the spot you're in to indulge the luxury of fear until later when your knees can safely turn to Jell-O—not far from where my legs were now.

5

THE BRIEFING

Fitting in

The final pre-trip meeting was held at a private social club, a cross between a bar and someone's living room. Most of the cyclists were there, along with the support people who would be traveling with us in vans—mostly drivers and wives who would procure our food on the road and help with logistics.

A buzz went around the room when we arrived. Word must have slipped out that Americans would be cycling with the group. Antonio introduced us, and announced that I would be cycling with the group as well. I would be the first woman, they thought, ever to travel on the bicycle with an Italian men's cycling group.

For an uncertain moment the room fell silent; they were non-plussed. My heart sank. I'd hoped they already knew I'd be pedaling with the group, not riding in one of the vans. Their surprised stares brought beads of sweat to my forehead, and my hands went clammy. I had a sudden awful feeling that Nino was enjoying my discomfort. I smiled at everyone to disguise my uneasiness and tried to look relaxed as I gazed around the room. The women nodded and smiled their approval, along with the organizers and some of the others. A few of the men could barely hide their shock and hostility; one macho-looking guy grimaced. My cheeks burned. I decided to seek out only friendly faces from then on. Nino broke the awkwardness of the moment by thanking them for inviting us and saying how much we were looking forward to joining the trip.

Antonio went over the specifics of the trip, and what kind of mileage and terrain we could expect. He said Luigi would be the cycling leader, but I couldn't see who he was. A large, ebullient man whom everyone addressed as "Dottore" boomed a few orders to the group. Nino glanced over and nodded to my unspoken query; this was the real boss.

The route for the trip had not been scouted, so the planning had been done on maps. No one in the group had actually traveled there before, since the borders into Czechoslovakia and Poland had opened only this year. We'd be the first cycling tour to cross into the former East in over forty years. The most direct route possible had been chosen commensurate with avoiding major highways except through Austria, where Dottore had routed us through some of his favorite regions.

Having a fair amount of experience getting lost on a bicycle, I knew that maps, no matter how good, always leave room for little surprises such as an occasionally unmarked killer grade, rerouted roads, detours, uncompleted roads that end unceremoniously in the middle of nowhere, sections where the pavement turns to gravel—but I tried to banish the thoughts. I'd just follow along and trust, even in the face of the tunnel episode, realizing this was the highest level of trust I'd ever had to have in a situation, especially due to my inability to understand anything being said.

We'd cover almost a thousand miles in ten days, without a rest day. When we reached Linz in northern Austria, we'd cycle north and cross into Eastern Europe at the Czechoslovakian border and then head northeast from Prague across the Carpathian Mountains into Poland, to Warsaw—only a hard day's ride from the Belarus border.

A Bicycle for Vaclav Havel

Dottore addressed the group about a very special bicycle we'd take as a gift to Vaclav Havel, the president of Czechoslovakia—a gesture of friendship from the Italians in the region of Verona. We'd cycle to the presidential palace in Prague and attempt to deliver it to him in person.

Dottore had telephoned to try to make an appointment for this. The message had been relayed to President Havel, who was an enthusiastic cyclist. He'd asked an aide to tell us that he wasn't sure he'd be in town on that date, but if he was, he'd be very happy to meet us and to receive the bicycle. No one had seen this special bicycle yet; it was stashed in one of the vans. It was a custom De Rosa, one of Italy's finest.

My Status

At the close of the meeting, when Nino was busy visiting with others, I took Antonio aside and paid my own cost for the trip, knowing this would not go unnoticed. Already I heard people referring to me as Nino's wife, and Nino not correcting them. I felt uneasy and confused that this bothered me, since the bloom on our relationship was still new and I was entertaining long-term thoughts about Nino. Besides paying lip service to Italian propriety, my sense was that he wanted the glory and credit of having a younger, vibrant "wife" who pedaled with the group. I didn't feel it had anything to do with me personally. It was a territory thing.

Funny, it never bothered me when we were checking into a hotel. But I'd committed to this trip as a cyclist, not as a wife. That was the part of me that paid Antonio for the trip where others could see, and that was the part of me that didn't like being treated as the invisible half of a couple. I pushed it out of my mind. For the moment.

6

THE START

Learning to Ride in the Pack

Cheers filled the air as Dottore announced the start and took the lead, followed by a small group of the faster elite riders. Many of the cyclists had already pushed off by the time I finished the TV interview for which I'd been so woefully unprepared. I scrambled onto my bike, and Nino and I set off at a comfortable pace; but my heart was racing and my skin prickled with excitement. I was already breathing hard, but so were the men; the sound of it, quickened by the excitement of the start, enfolded me. A sea of leg muscles strained, tires crunched on the road. *Please, God, don't let me make a fool of myself in front of all these men. Give me the strength to do this, and so help me I'll never ask for another thing* (soon I learned not to make promises like this).

The men were chatting happily, reaching out to put a hand on a friend's shoulder as they rode, and shouting greetings to friends. The group spread out on the road west to the Adige River, the strongest cyclists in front and the rest of us spread out over half a kilometer or so. A rush of cool air washed over us as we reached the river and turned north up the Val d'Adige toward the Brenner Pass.

Opera music began to play full blast over a megaphone speaker mounted on top of one of the vans, and the glorious tenor voice of

Pavarotti reverberated up and down my spine as it echoed across the river, thrilling my whole being with the complete joy of the moment. I threw back my head and laughed; Italians really knew how to make the most of their moments. A few of the men started to sing robustly along with the aria as we pedaled and drank in the mist-laden, cool morning air by the river, celebrating our presence in the world on the beginning of this great adventure.

I rode with Nino, Dino, and Guido, who had joined us for the first leg of the trip and would cycle with us only as far north as Bolzano. Guido had taken it upon himself to help me as much as possible. The pace had picked up now, and was evening out at about eighteen miles per hour. It was too fast for me, and I labored to keep up.

Guido pulled up alongside and told me again how important it was for me to draft in order to stay with the pack. "Let the leaders break the wind, and your pedaling will be twenty percent easier," he told me. "Try not to cycle between groups, as I saw you do earlier. Don't change gears so often, either; it's too hard on your legs. Find your place in the pack and your optimum gear, and stick with it."

I listened carefully, grateful for his help. Again he admonished me, "Remember when you're drafting someone, to spin at the same rate in exactly the gear they are in. If they stand, you stand. If they sit, you sit; that way you'll be able to stay with them. Stick to them like glue."

"Okay," I shouted to him above the wind and the sound of the male Italian voices all around me. "I'll do it."

"And another thing," he raised his voice above the din, "not everyone will want you to draft them. Watch for a sign that it's okay with them for you to be on their wheel." He went on, "And ride steady, hold your line. The men will be grateful for your stability on the bike, as you'll be grateful for theirs. That's how to be safe riding in a pack. Signal to those in back of you if you'll be moving to the right or to the left, or slowing down." Then he said, "Watch me," as he moved ahead and demonstrated.

This was the first time I'd cycled in a pack, and I hadn't experienced before how close together we'd ride. They rode so close I could smell their breath. I could see now how imperative it was that everybody hold their line, signal to move, and play by the same rules. I had to trust them, and they had to trust me.

I thanked God for Guido. What a gift his instruction was. I looked over at Nino to see if he was listening to any of this. He was busy chatting with Dino; this was of no interest to him.

Finally I had to find a bathroom. Nino and Dino stopped with me at a gas station. I'd already seen men stopped at the side of the road to pee. I envied their ease of solving the problem, vowing to limit myself to one cup of coffee in the morning for the duration of the trip.

Now we were behind the pack, and pedaled hard to catch up. We never did, but we eventually came upon them at the first rest stop.

The wives who were accompanying us were passing out rolls. There were six of them. A jolly-looking group, they chatted amiably. No English here, either. I introduced myself as best I could.

"One of them said, "*Brava, Lina!*"

Nino and Lina, fresh as daisies

"*Grazie*," I smiled, looking forward to visiting with them, in spite of our language barriers. By the time I'd assembled my meat and cheese on the roll, some of the cyclists were already getting ready to shove off. The parking area where we'd stopped was still fringed with the backs of men peeing in the bushes. Privacy was obviously not an issue for Italian male cyclists. I could see at these rest stops there would be time for me either to eat or to relieve myself, but not both. How would I ever handle this? Remembering the time it took to get the key, I knew the gas station option was out. So I'd have to use the bushes too—and not before any prying male eyes, either. Well, I'd figure it out, somehow. I gulped down a couple of bites of the *panino*, shoved the rest of it into my jersey pocket, and set off with the group.

7

Day One: Verona to Chiusa, 105 miles

Meeting the Men

Pedaling along with the group, always just a little faster than was comfortable for me, I started to think about pacing myself and saving some of my strength for later in the day when I'd really need it. I waited for the pain in my legs from the fast pace to subside. It never did—an ever-present reminder that they were stronger than I was.

I'd always believed that strength depended upon the person, not upon the gender. But pedaling now with the men, I was forced to admit they really were stronger. I knew that men enjoyed a twenty percent greater muscle-to-fat ratio than women, but the knowledge had been intellectual. Now I was experiencing it; their stronger legs could push higher gears, putting their front wheel a little farther ahead of mine with every pedal stroke. I wondered if the pain in my legs from the speed would go away, and I tried not to think about how I'd endure it for the whole trip. I looked for ways not to be discouraged. With training, I knew I could be stronger than some of them, but that was of little solace now.

I found myself cycling in a group of men I didn't know. Dino and Guido were ahead, but Nino was nowhere to be seen. The men were talking animatedly, gesturing with their hands in the Italian way as they rode. It was fun to watch them, one hand on the handlebars and the other jabbing at the air, making a point. Most were tall, lean, and bursting with male exuberance.

The sexes seemed more polarized in Italy, the men more masculine, the women more feminine. I wondered if this was because the sex roles here were so separate and distinct, while in America men and women shared more of the same roles and chores both at home and in business. But for now I was enveloped in a completely male energy field, and I loved it.

Despite a constant, nagging dread that I'd be left behind, I was enjoying myself immensely. The day couldn't have been more perfect; the June sun, filtered through a mild haze, warmed my back, and the river cooled the air. I'd fall back on rises and then have to pedal hard to move forward to my original position. If I kept falling back I'd fall off the back of the pack, and I wanted to feel the security of knowing there were still cyclists behind me.

Laboring up one such rise, suddenly I felt a hand on my back; someone was pushing me. I was astonished, never having experienced this practice at home. I couldn't turn around to look, not wanting to waver from my line. At the top of the rise the hand disappeared, and I looked around to see a tall, very thin man in his late fifties, with a tanned and weathered face.

"*Mi chiamo* Umberto," ("My name is Umberto") he said. I thanked him, grateful but not at all sure if I wanted these episodes to become a habit. He pointed to my gears and began to speak to me in Italian. I shrugged that I couldn't speak Italian, and he understood.

He held up one finger and pointed to my gears and the shifters. He held up three and then four fingers, pointed to my legs, shook his head violently, and feigned tiredness.

"Okay," I said, guessing he meant I should stay in one gear.

Another cyclist came alongside and introduced himself. His name was Bruno, and he would be the only one besides Guido who spoke a little English. He had kind blue eyes and a gentle manner. He didn't appear to have the aggressive style of male cyclists who have cycled competitively, but I noticed he spun his pedals fast and seemed skilled and steady. I hoped to learn more about him. He tried to tell me about his family, mixing English and Italian. He was very proud of them, and his love for them was apparent in his eyes as he spoke.

I told him about my own two grown sons, but it was hard to talk since I needed all of my breath to keep up. He understood, and we pedaled along in silence for awhile, taking in the beautiful Val d'Adige.

As we passed through the village of Borghetto, Bruno made me understand in spite of our lack of mutually understood words, that this town, the border to the Trentino region to the north, had once been the border between Italy and Austria. Later I learned that the borders had been redrawn after World War I when this region had been ceded to Italy as the spoils of war. Now the region enjoyed a semiautonomous status, but many of the people retained their Austrian cultural identity, and spoke as much German as Italian.

The road we were on was the secondary highway heading north toward the Brenner Pass. It was lightly traveled and had an ample shoulder. Beside us, the Adige River ran through the broad, flat valley. As we pedaled, we were surrounded by vineyards interspersed with vegetable gardens, giving the valley the look of a richly colored, many-hued tapestry. The sides of the valley rose abruptly to high ridges which steepened, as we traveled north, to become the Tyrol to the northwest and the Dolomites to the northeast. Bruno tapped me on the shoulder and pointed to a monastery tucked high on a ridge to the west.

He crossed himself, and then asked me, "Are you religious?"

"Yes," I answered, "but I'm not a Catholic."

"Oh," he said, looking confused. Later I learned when an Italian in Italy asks if you are religious, they want to know if you're a good

Catholic. Bruno told me that many people make a hiking pilgrimage up the mountain to that place every year, and he had done it many times.

Occasionally an immense fortress came into view. These had been built high on bluffs over the river during the Middle Ages to guard the valley from invading tribes from the north. The Brenner Pass was one of the most important routes into Italy from the north, and each fortress had represented a different fiefdom.

The sight of the massive stone walls and parapets made those medieval times seem like yesterday. What must it have been like to have been a woman, holed up forever in one of those places? God, how lucky I am to have my precious freedom.

Sometimes a village would be tucked into the foot of a ridge at the edge of the valley. The earth-hued buildings and red tile roofs made the village appear pink in the distance, against the dark green backdrop of the forest that climbed part-way up the ridge, until it became too steep to hold soil. The village was always presided over by the church steeple, giving it an aura of settled peace.

It was a funny thing about seeing all this from the seat of a bicycle. Traveling by car, it was easy to take the scenery for granted, and you always had the impression that you were seeing someone else's world. On a bicycle, it was my world. I was part of the countryside and shared my identity with the people there. I saw myself hoeing with the man in his garden, cooking with his wife in the kitchen, or sipping a cappuccino in the café that would be in the little piazza. I never tried to imagine these things; they just popped into my mind. Over every little rise was a different world of which I was a part. How could anyone ever get bored on a bicycle?

Bruno tapped me on the shoulder to tell me we'd stop for lunch in the town we were approaching. Suddenly I was hungry, and remembered the *panino* I had in my pocket from the last rest stop. I'd never eaten while pedaling, and I looked forward to eating the *panino* sitting down on something other than a bicycle seat.

We were gradually starting to climb now, and the mountains were coming closer into view. We were approaching Trento, the gateway to the mountains. The Brenner Pass to Austria lay a day ahead to the north.

Trento is a mountain town, and also a busy provincial center. Everything seemed vertical, with old, multistoried buildings rising from the edges of narrow, cobbled streets, church steeples and mountains looming overhead. The pace of life was leisurely. Young mothers were out in the new warmth of the late morning, a baguette stuck in the baby's stroller, greeting neighbors. Here and there shutters needed fixing and plaster had fallen off some walls, revealing older, richer colors underneath. Sometimes gay designs were painted in a band around the top of a house. You could tell by the contented expression on people's faces that life worked here.

Approaching the hill where the group had congregated for lunch, I was absorbed in the life of the town. Suddenly a large, strong hand connected with the middle of my back like an electric shock. Startled, I almost lost my balance. Without warning or a how-do-you-do, someone was sweeping me up the short, steep hill, as if I'd been in the way. By the time I got around to thinking, *Who the hell does he think he is?* and looked around to see who it was, we'd arrived.

He didn't stop, speak, smile, or look at me as he passed me to join his friends.

My God, who was that? I could still feel the imprint of his hand on my back. The power in his hand coursed through me, and seemed to reach out far beyond him. Whoever he was, he had about the same regard for me as he'd have for a bug. I was still trying to figure out how to react when Nino found me. "Who is that?" I asked him, pointing to the tall, unsmiling, intense man who had pushed me up the hill.

"That's Luigi, the cycling leader. I understand he was a famous racer—one of the best." The men congregated around him, vying for his attention. He was tall, lean, and unsmiling, with straight, graying black hair. He had long legs on which he stalked about restlessly.

Nino said, "I've heard the men talking about him. No one seems to be neutral about Luigi. Either they love him or they hate him."

"Why?" I asked.

"They say he's a loner, that he's never been a team player. But they all say he had more raw talent than anyone; his climbing skills are legendary. They say that without a sponsor or a team, he won race after race, becoming one of the best. But I've also heard him called a dark horse and a loose cannon—not a man I'd want to trust," he added.

I watched Luigi as I munched on the remainder of my *panino* while I waited for the crowd to thin out around the lunch table. I was fascinated with the bearing and easy grace with which he carried himself. Just watching him, I knew he wouldn't care what people said about him. He was his own man, comfortable in his skin.

Tearing my gaze away, I excused myself to find a bathroom. No bushes here. By the time I returned, they were all ready to go again, Luigi looking impatient and annoyed in the lead. *God, how will I eat? How will I solve this problem?* I grabbed a banana, a roll, and a hunk of cheese and shoved off, this time with Nino.

The uphill stretches came more often now. I forced myself to eat between them, when it was flat and I didn't have to breathe so hard. Chew it well so you can digest it, I admonished myself. Boy, this really was food-as-fuel. But I didn't care. I loved the ceremony of a meal, but now all I wanted was to keep up my strength.

Nino dropped back to pedal with Antonio, and I was alone between groups. Tiring, I tried not to slow down. We'd been on the road for seven hours. Suddenly, a crack of thunder made me jump. The sky had been blue just a few minutes ago. How could this be? A thunderstorm was rolling in behind us, and it started to rain. Everyone stopped to put on rain jackets, and by the time we got back on our bikes, it was pouring.

A Little Help from My Friends

Pedaling on in the downpour, I felt the water thrown up by my wheels begin to soak my socks. "God, why would you do this to me when I'm so tired and it's all uphill?"

My guardian angel, Angelo, suddenly appeared. "*Because that's life, kid,*" he said. "*Put your legs on automatic. You don't have far to go.*"

"Oh, okay, Angelo. Nice to see you. Wondered if you were along."

"*I'm always along, kid.*"

Angelo appeared for the first time when I was exploring the Provence region of France alone on my bicycle. Thinking back on it, I was pretty sure I hadn't just conjured him up. One day, far out in the rural countryside, I'd become lost. Suddenly he was just there. I found it odd he was Italian, since I wasn't Italian myself and had never been to Italy. He sat on my left shoulder. He was about six inches high, with a slight build, and slicked-back, black hair.

"*Ciao, kid,*" he introduced himself. "*I'm Angelo.*"

"Oh, hi," I responded, somewhat startled.

"*Don't sweat it,*" he said. "*Retrace your steps to the last set of direction signs.*"

Of course! Why hadn't I thought of that? Angelo proved to be a man—an angel—of few words, for an Italian. He was pretty short on sympathy, and not beyond a little sarcasm. He'd jab my shoulder with his heel when a car would pass too close. "*Hey! Pay attention! How can I do my job if you don't do yours?*"

After that, Angelo always appeared when I needed him.

Watching the big wet drops pelt my shorts, I wondered how long my nether parts would stay dry. Umberto pedaled alongside me, pointing to an old house up ahead on the left side of the road. A few cyclists had already stopped there, seeking shelter from the storm. The house seemed deserted, and we huddled together under the protection of the eaves. Our differences were fewer now, since we were all covered with the same muddy road dirt.

Through the straining boughs of a wind-whipped aspen, I caught filtered glimpses of an ancient stone castle, perched high on a grassy slope of the steepening Alps. A young German couple huddled with us for shelter, and I could smell the earthy wet leather of their motorcycle jackets.

As suddenly as it had begun, the storm was over.

Umberto told me we had only twenty kilometers to go. How could I go the full 105 miles today, when so far I only had a sixty-mile body? Utterly spent, the fatigue and the continual pain in my legs made me cry as I pedaled. Thankful my glasses covered my face, I prayed no one would notice. Someone must have played a cruel joke and attached a fifty-pound weight to each of my pedals.

It was all uphill now. As I strained to put one pedal in front of the other, Umberto put his hand to my back, pushed me for eight seconds or so, and then gave me a mighty shove. He'd waited to push me until he could see I really needed it. His hand infused me with new strength, made me know I'd make it. Finally Chiusa, our destination for the day, came into view. Somehow I got there.

We were still in Italy, but you couldn't prove it by the town of Chiusa. It was an alpine village with cobbled streets and Austrian chalets. Local people wore Tyrolean hats and knickers, and carried mountain walking sticks to get around the steep streets of the town. More like Austrians than Italians, they were conservative people, and appeared more than a little taken aback at the loud swarm of happy cyclists congregating in the small piazza beside our hotel.

I don't know how I did it—105 miles! My legs almost buckled as I got off my bicycle. They shook and ached, and I was sure I couldn't have made it another ten yards. I sat on the ledge of the piazza fountain next to Nino, waiting to see what would happen next. We exchanged glances. I saw the lines of fatigue on his face; he was as tired as I was.

He beamed at me. "Bless your heart, you made it!"

I squeezed his arm affectionately, basking in his pride. I pulled off the soaked bandanna from around my forehead and wiped my red eyes with it, dropping my hair-matted head between my knees in a moment of blissful relaxation. The air rang with cyclists congratulating each other—"*Complimenti! Complimenti!*"—on the successful completion of our first day.

Ponte per l'Europa Unita

Dinner at our quaint, old-world hotel was five courses, including three separate kinds of pasta in one course, each more mouth-watering than the last. We sat with Antonio and Dottore, who asked Nino to translate and explain to me the underlying purpose of our trip.

For the first years after World War II, there was no contact between Italy and neighboring countries to the north. Antagonisms were still left from the war. It was a time of facing inward, of rebuilding at home. So, to reduce tensions, the region of Verona adopted a sister city program. Engelheim am Rhein in Austria was selected as the sister city for San Pietro in Cariano, because they were both wine-producing communities. A few years after the war, Dottore led a trip to the new sister city; he and a group from Verona would go by bicycle. The trip would be an exchange of friendship and a time of healing, exorcizing ghosts of the war. For most of the riders, this would be their first trip, by bicycle, outside of Italy.

When Dottore and his group arrived, the people of Engelheim received them with great fanfare and joy. With speeches proclaiming new bonds of friendship, a great flower crown was placed on Dottore's bicycle, and everyone celebrated their hopes for an open, postwar Europe, bringing friendship, trade, prosperity, and peace.

Now in 1990, Dottore and a new group from the Verona region, including a few of the original members, would venture by bicycle into Eastern Europe, where borders were being opened for the first time as the Iron Curtain lifted, creaking with the rust of a failed system. Today, the goal was more than friendship. The Italians had a dream of being goodwill ambassadors to help create a *"ponte per l'Europa unita,"* a bridge for a united Europe.

Although Dottore and Antonio loved the sport of cycling, they said the bicycle was for them simply the best way to travel and see the world. They loved seeing the countryside in the companionship of our group. The most important thing for them, they said, was to establish links of friendship with people in the countries we visited. They looked forward to seeing the ways of life of other people, to celebrate our differences, our similarities, and our common bonds. Glasses were refilled, and we drank a toast to the *ponte per l'Europa unita.*

After dinner, arm in arm, Nino and I strolled around the town. Small shops were built right to the edge of crooked cobblestone lanes, their windows filled with colorful, handcrafted toys. It was a quiet village, shaded and dominated by the mountains. An old castle, now a nunnery, was perched high above the town. On the down slope were community vegetable gardens planted in narrow rows interspersed with flowers, carefully tended. Geraniums in all shades of red and pink filled the window boxes of the chalet-style houses. The signs were in German as well as Italian. Not many people were out; a man wearing lederhosen and a Tyrolean hat and carrying a walking stick nodded a greeting to us. It was a separate mountain world.

In the warm bed at last, I swept aside any doubts I was having about Nino and about my ability to keep up. We slept close together under eiderdowns covered with crisp fresh sheets that smelled of the sun.

8

Day Two: Chiusa to Stans, Austria, 80 miles

The Brenner Pass

Today we'd climb the Brenner Pass. I'd been pedaling up the switchbacks in my dream. Opening my eyes, the dream's vision came into my full consciousness. I didn't know the climb had been so much on my mind; it took everything I had just to live in the moment. In fact, I'd made an effort not to think about it.

As I luxuriated in the early morning feeling of the soft eiderdown, my thoughts drifted back to dinner the night before. The pasta was the best I'd ever tasted. I wished I'd been able to understand the jokes at which they all laughed so uproariously, but I never had so much fun with a bunch of people I couldn't understand. They bellowed at each other in great friendship as they consumed unbelievable quantities of food, which kept appearing from apparently bottomless pots in the kitchen. Although I was dying to talk to people, it was nice, when I was so tired, not to have to.

Sitting up in bed, I put on my glasses and started to write in my journal. Soon Dino knocked and entered in his pajamas to talk to Nino, while others wrapped in towels or in other states of partial undress poked their heads in to say, "*Buon Giorno*! *Come va*, Lina?" ("Good morning! How goes it, Lina?") It was like a big fraternity house, and somehow I felt right at home holding court in bed, in my glasses and nightshirt.

At breakfast, I kept hearing the word "*percento*"—they were talking about the steepness of the grade ahead. I decided not to inquire, preferring to take it as it came. Nino volunteered that there would be one steep, three-kilometer section (about two miles) called the Colle (mountain pass or hill) Isarco. He said it had been suggested that I ride in one of the vans that day.

"No thanks, I want to try," I said, knowing I'd do more than try.

Nino told me this would be the hardest day of the trip. I began to wish he wouldn't tell me stuff like that. I'm sure he didn't realize that remarks like that took potshots at my confidence. We'd cycle up the Brenner Pass at 1,375 meters (4,530 feet), climbing more than 3,000 feet for the day. Then we'd cross over into Austria at the top of the pass, descend to Innsbruck and cycle east to the small village of Stans, San Pietro in Cariano's sister city.

Nino and I started out at eight o'clock with the early group, led by Dottore. He'd invited us to cycle with him so he could show us our first sight of the Dolomites. The village was still asleep as we quietly pulled out. The only sound was the "bump, bump" of our skinny tires on the cobblestones and the "whoosh" we made as we met the cold morning breeze, wending our way through the quiet village streets.

The ascent started right away. It was a steady climb as the road became long switchbacks into the mountains, and we were able to keep a good rhythm. I was learning that the rhythm of the pedaling created a momentum that itself helped you to keep doing it. Every day I tried to find my rhythm, to put my body into a physical harmony with the pedaling.

I pedaled with Dottore, Nino, and Bruno. We didn't talk, immersed in the quiet of the morning, the rhythm of the sustained effort, the quiet rolling of our tires, the ever-present song of the wind in the tall trees. As we proceeded up the long switchbacks, we could look down on cyclists coming up behind us. When they passed us, I could pick out the words, "*dura*" ("hard") and "*ripida*" ("steep"), from snatches of conversation drifting back about the Colle Isarco, looming ahead.

Occasionally one of the vans waited on a curve. The driver and the women took pictures and shouted encouragement, "*Bravo! Bravo!*" And, "*Brava, Lina!*"

And so we proceeded up through the lush and green Val d'Adige, which gradually became the deep valley of the Brenner. As the valley narrowed, the slopes appeared bathed in green grass and patches of forest. Chalets and occasional small hamlets were perched on the steep slopes. Through clefts at the tops of the ridges, we caught glimpses of the elusive, stark peaks of the Dolomites to the east.

My bicycle and I melted into the countryside, alive and vibrant with mountain meadows of lupine and buttercups. The sky was a deep, clear blue, and the cool mountain air caressed us as we pedaled. The oncoming Isarco River rushed down beside us, sometimes bathing our faces in a welcome mist. I loved the sound of the river; it was a voice of the earth.

We arrived at the rest stop at Vipiteno well behind the others. The men studied me out of the corners of their eyes to see how tired I was. Self-conscious, I almost fell getting off my bicycle on shaky legs while trying to look spry and energetic. I smiled at my new friends, not acknowledging their concerned looks. Umberto came over, and reaching for my bike, said in Italian that he would put my bicycle in the van.

I got it immediately. I hung on to my bicycle and said, "*Absoluta-mente* not!" not knowing if *absolutamente* really was a word. (It was.)

Several of the men had come over, saying, "*Si! Si!*"

I shouted back, "No! No!" as someone propelled me toward the van, still maintaining a vise-like grip on my bike. Not accustomed to being propelled, I was so surprised I hardly knew what to do. Balking like a stubborn mule came to mind, so that's what I did. Remembering what Nino told me about the 'no riding in the van' rule, I was afraid if I let them put me in the van, they wouldn't let me ride again. Dottore came over, and all activity stopped as he stood with hands on his hips, contemplating me. Finally he told them I should have my chance to pedal, and they left me. Nino watched all this without intervening. Why didn't he come to my defense? Although reason told me there was nothing he could have done, I felt suddenly very alone in my endeavor.

The reason for all the fuss was we were about to begin the ascent of the Colle Isarco. They said it would be seven to fourteen percent, and I couldn't possibly do it. The steepest part would be for only three kilometers, and only sixteen kilometers (ten miles) remained now to the top of the Brenner.

Mario came over, and pointed to a bicycle on top of one of the vans, with a granny gear. I agreed to take it, relieved to have a bike with lower gears.

Nino looked on as Mario unloaded the bike, and I knew he would have preferred that I'd gone in the van. I found myself wishing he'd join the others leaving now, so I could do it by myself. *Oh, stop it*, I told myself. *He's just concerned for your safety.*

I watched the men leaving and knew I'd have no time to eat, again. I stuffed an apple and a roll in my pocket; I could eat them when the ascent lessened. *For cryin' out loud*, I thought, in angry frustration at my own lack of ability to keep up, *what's your big hurry?*

Mario lowered the bike seat as far as it would go, and Nino and I set off. The damn thing was so big I could hardly pedal it, and the saddle was a rock-like wedge. Taking it had been a mistake, but I figured I could handle it for ten miles.

The grade became steep even before we left town. The road was very narrow and winding, with no shoulder. The valley narrowed to a gorge, and the roaring rapids of the Isarco River rushed angrily toward us beside the road. The grade was indeed seven to fourteen percent, very steep.

Rounding a bend, my chain slipped off the chain ring as I shifted gears on the unfamiliar bike. Nino said, "You know, you can prevent that by not yanking the gears."

My anger flashed. I'd been annoyed with him before, but not like this. A picture popped into my head of hoisting my bike over my head and bashing him with it. Whammo! "Don't you think I know that, for God's sake?" I shouted, waving my arms, Italian style. I hooked the chain back onto the chain ring, wiped my greasy fingers on some weeds and my shorts, and we continued on our way, Nino suffering silently with his best *I-try-so-hard-but-you-can-never-please-them* pout. Just as well—we needed all our breath to pedal.

Then Nino had a flat. I watched as he sweated and swore while he ineptly changed the tube. Nino was a financial wizard, but he was not good at fixing flats. I suppressed an urge to do it for him, and bit my tongue to prevent myself from telling him he wouldn't get so many flats if he'd keep more air in his tires. I was beginning to realize that even though he was stronger, I was the more skilled cyclist.

I said, "Please go ahead. I'll be slower, and I can do it better if I keep my own pace." Glad to be pedaling alone, I prayed, sweated, breathed, ground away, and thrilled to the falling rapids beside me. I looked for my rhythm, but I was pedaling too slowly to find it. I put my full consciousness and everything else I had into each pedal stroke. It was just plain hard. Finally the gorge opened up and the steepness abated. With a flood of relief I realized that the worst of it was behind me. Soon I caught up to Nino and we were chatting again.

Eventually we found ourselves pedaling along beside the auto-strada. Traffic was backed up for a kilometer, waiting to cross into

Austria at the border checkpoint. We pedaled past one of our vans that had been hanging back waiting for us. I realized we'd taken this van away from the group, away from other cyclists who might have needed help. This reminded me anew I'd have to do better, to keep up, somehow.

We found our group in the parking lot just before the border crossing. A few of the men applauded when I pedaled in, and one of them handed me a bouquet of wildflowers. The women clapped and called to me, "*Brava, Lina!*" I basked in the attention, not caring it would probably spoil me for normal life forever. Wine was being dispensed from one of the vans, rolls and cheese were being munched, and cyclists were milling about. I changed bicycles, wishing I could change bodies. I decided never to give up my bike again.

Longing for a cup of coffee, I caught it's wonderful, rich aroma wafting through the air. I followed my nose and found three big espresso pots brewing, perched on propane camp stoves on the ground by one of vans. The pots were surrounded by a dozen caffeine-addicted cyclists, shot-size paper cups in hand, waiting expectantly. Italians tend to drink their coffee like Americans down a shot of whiskey. Lord, it was strong! I shuddered as it went down and found myself downing it in a gulp, like they did.

Almost Downhill into Austria

As we mounted up to cross the border, Dottore thundered to us that we would *not* descend the Brenner Pass like a bunch of screaming banshees, as he knew we'd do if left to our own devices. We'd follow the lead van, he admonished, which would go no faster than twenty-eight miles per hour, and anyone who passed it wouldn't be allowed to come on any future trips. He said we had to get permission from the Austrian police to pass through Austria, and they were *not* fond of large groups of cyclists, especially Italians. Everyone grumbled; cyclists do not like to be robbed of the earned thrills of their descents.

Cycling up the Brenner

Soon after we crossed the border, we came upon a long tunnel. The police were motioning that we couldn't go through the tunnel, but must take the narrow, steep road over the top. I fell behind once again on the steep ascent, even with the help of a kind hand that gave me an occasional push. I looked around and saw it was Bruno, smiling his encouragement.

We stopped for a breather at the top. Nino told me, "Luigi and some of the men are complaining about having to wait for *"La Americana."* Why did he have to tell me the demoralizing things? Whenever he made a negative remark it affected my strength. I didn't want to be a pain in the ass to these men; it was their trip, after all. I'd try to do better—no!—I *would* do better.

From the start, a few of the men didn't hide their hostility toward my cycling with the group. Their glares made no secret of their attitude that a woman had no place cycling with the men. By now I knew who these were and made an effort to avoid looking at them, to keep their bad feelings from affecting me, weakening me. Instead I concentrated on those whom I had befriended.

So that was what they called me: "*La Americana.*" It made me feel proud, but the impersonal nature of it made me feel like a nonperson. I made a mental note to tell Luigi my name.

Fortunately my downhill skills were a lot better than my uphill skills, so catching up with King Luigi and the Knights was no problem. Skiing had been my lifelong sport. I'd raced in the downhill as a teenager, and later in the slalom and giant slalom. The balance and rhythm of descending on a bicycle was not unlike skiing (except that pavement is a lot harder than snow), and the thrill of the speed was the cycling reward I lived for. Noting I was out of the line of Dottore's sight and knowing I could plead ignorance of the language, I felt redeemed as I went into a tuck and sped downhill, passing many of the surprised men. But my enjoyment of the moment was short-lived as I caught up with the van and it became necessary to ride single file at a uniform speed.

The descent was miles long, on the twisting, two-lane road. It was Sunday, and it seemed that half of Austria was returning from their weekend in Italy. Motorcycle after motorcycle passed us, a hundred or more, in a never-ending stream. As I rode the narrow shoulder, two motorcycles roared along beside me, abreast, and another was passing them, all on the right side of the road. The nearest one was only three feet away. I was dying to study the riders—their looks, their manner, their clothes, their vehicles—but I dared not lift my eyes from the road or distract my peripheral vision to see how anyone else was doing, except to hold my line and keep a safe distance from the cyclist in front of me, as we snaked down the Brenner in the whine of the wind and hundreds of engines, a bunch of adventuring fools, all. I can't remember ever being happier.

At the bottom of the descent, we formed a pack, and traveled very fast. Drafting one or another in the middle of the pack, I thanked God for Guido's instructions. It was too fast for me, but I knew I had to stay with them. The pain in my legs was at the borderline of what I could tolerate. I didn't know where Nino was and I had a nagging fear of being left behind. If I dropped off the back, I'd never catch up.

I didn't understand the need I had to do this. But now it defined me, and I just kept putting one foot in front of the other, thrilled to the core to be there, doing it.

Soon we could see the multistoried buildings of Innsbruck, surrounded by high mountains cradling a wide valley, under a perfectly blue sky. In town, I thanked God for the stoplights.

We stopped at a park for lunch. In short order the wives had tables set up and were passing out rolls. I hadn't noticed it before, but a commercial deli meat slicer was rolled out of one of the vans on a custom ramp somebody had made for that purpose, and Italian meats and cheeses were being sliced for our *panini* (sandwiches). Everyone was in high spirits, knowing we didn't have far to go. They joked and laughed, and teased each other mercilessly as corks popped from special stashes of wine. For the first time I noticed the five-gallon containers in the back of one of the vans; someone was dispensing wine from one by way of a siphon hose. So we had one van for repairs, one for the food, and one for the wine. How very Italian!

Wine never seemed to affect Nino's abilities, and he was something of a connoisseur. He brought us both a cup of wine. I took one sip and caught Bruno's eye, who was waving his forefinger back and forth and shaking his head. I laughed, knowing he was right, and gave the wine back to Nino.

The men were more used to me now, and I could wander around, visiting, without attracting so much attention as before. I began to relax and have fun, using my first words in Italian conversation. They would ask me, "*Lina! Lina! Come va?*" ("Lina, how goes it?") or "*Tutto* okay?" and I would say, "*Si! Si!*" or "*Bene! Bene!*" ("Fine!") They seemed to say everything twice, so I did too.

The last miles to the village of Stans were relatively flat, enabling me to admire the rich color of the afternoon sun on the snow-capped Alps across the valley. As we cycled up into a small park in the center of the village, tubas, trumpets, and trombones of the town's brass band welcomed us with a robust march. The town officials were all

Lina

out to meet us, including Ludwig, Dottore's friend and mayor of the town. There was a great feast of sandwiches, fruit, and cold cuts.

Dottore motioned for us to join him in the beer garden with the mayor and his friends. He pulled me down beside him and explained me in German to the curious group; God only knows what he was saying. Then he made me stand up, and he poked my legs to show off my muscles. His audience *ooh*ed and *aah*ed and giggled as I sputtered, "*Dottore! Per favore, no!*" Fortunately no one spoke English, so I was relieved of having to articulate further. But I knew he really was proud of me, so I took it all in good stride. When you were Dottore, you could get away with practically anything.

After dinner we were treated to a show of Austrian singing, dancing, and yodeling. Dottore, feeling no pain, whisked me onto the dance floor for a polka. I did my best, not knowing how to polka, and at least we remained upright, and everyone applauded mightily—for the effort and exuberance, I supposed. For a minute there, I forgot I was tired.

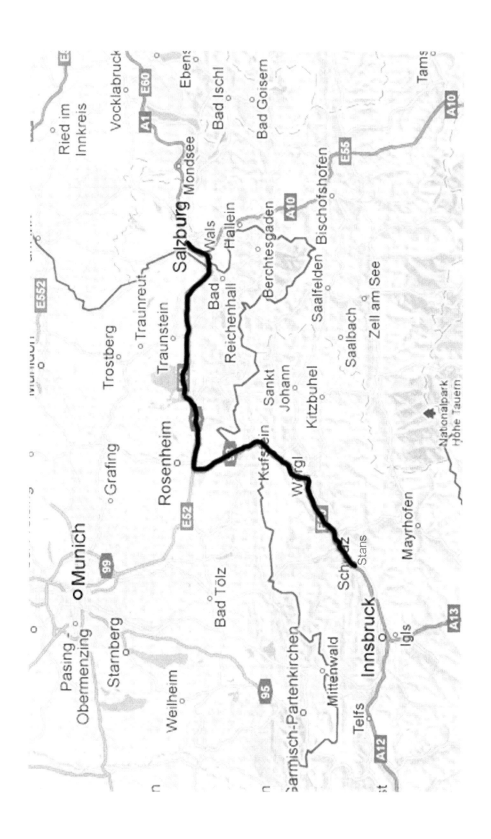

9

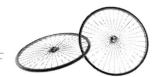

DAY THREE: STANS TO SALZBURG, 86 MILES

Finding my Place in the Pack

Over an abundant buffet-style Austrian breakfast, the men talked about how much easier today would be. I'd learned from experience that all cyclists are liars when it comes to telling you how easy something is, and I figured this was no exception. Today we'd go eighty-six miles, and if you believed you could go eighty-six flat miles in the Austrian Alps, then I had a bridge to sell you.

Nino told me how easy the day would be, and it amused me to watch myself listening to him. My female inclination was to believe everything he said, especially since he had such an air of absolute authority. I didn't think he affected it; it was just natural for him. Since we'd met, I'd believed whatever words had fallen from his knowing lips, and I was always surprised when he'd been mistaken about something. I smiled as he recounted the details of the day ahead, knowing he'd never been where we were going before, either.

"What's so damn funny?" he demanded.

"Hey, I just think you're cute," I said. I did, too. But now, when my welfare and even survival depended upon it, I filed what he said in what I had dubbed "Nino's Bum Dope Drawer," and decided to assess for myself whether I thought it would be an easy day. I did not. Out of Nino's earshot, I asked Bruno if he thought it would be an easy day, the first of many second opinions I would furtively seek. He did not, either.

We had no sooner hit the road at eight, our usual starting time, when we turned off again into what looked like someone's garden. It was someone's garden; our host must have invited us the night before. All smiles, he emerged from his large chalet with a giant tray full of shot glasses filled with grappa, which he passed around. I supposed he thought this would get us off to a good start. Though many of the men downed theirs as if this was their normal macho morning fare, I saw a few glances of dismay exchanged, and followed Bruno's lead as he and a few others dumped theirs surreptitiously into beds of petunias. We milled around for awhile, and finally were on our way.

Everything in the countryside looked shiny, clean, and prosperous. Snow clung to gullies in the jagged peaks of the Alps. The green mountain slopes were dotted with chalets, their window boxes overflowing with geraniums.

The keynote for Austria was orderliness. Somehow its predictability detracted from the great beauty of the place. The chalets were all white, fields perfectly rectangular, rows of vegetables straight, geraniums uniformly red. Austria was a gorgeous country, but I had an inexplicable urge to tip over a garbage can. I preferred the sensuous disorderliness of Italy, where a woman might be screaming out a window at her wayward husband, or lovers might be kissing in the shadows.

In spite of my judgmental attitude I was enjoying myself immensely, watching the rural countryside fly by. Cycling with Dottore, who loved Austria and loved showing it to us, I listened wistfully as he extolled the virtues of the country. I just wished I could understand what he was saying.

After awhile I pedaled on ahead to remove myself from the stress of never being able to understand what was being said. Sometimes it got to me, and I had to get away from it. Smiling, I remembered the night at the posh Verona restaurant when I'd tried to order more bread.

When Nino and I had first arrived in Italy, we disagreed about food-ordering policy in restaurants. To my great surprise, he'd order for me without asking what I wanted to eat, which he never did at home. I convinced him it was appropriate for me to make my own menu selections; but then he didn't listen when I told him what I wanted to eat, and he'd still order the wrong thing. If I corrected his order in front of the (male) Italian (career) waiter, they'd both glare at me as if I were rude beyond redemption. So I'd insisted on ordering my own food, and doggedly memorized a few words from my Italian menu-master. I'd pestered poor Nino, "How do you say 'I'd like to have,' or 'please bring me'?" and "What's the word for …?"

One evening at dinner I'd asked the waiter, "*Cameriere, vorrei piu pene.*" I meant *pane* (bread). Simple. "Waiter, I'd like more bread." Instead I'd said, "Waiter, I'd like more penis."

A shocked hush fell over the restaurant. Nino put his elbows on the table and hid his face in his hands. Finally he peeked out between his fingers, revealing one tired brown eye twitching in humiliation. "*Pane!* Not *pene!* *Pane!*" he whispered hoarsely. "You just asked for more penis. God, I'll never be able to come back here."

"Oh." What more was there to say?

Now my thoughts turned to Dottore; I hoped he wasn't upset that I'd passed him today. When he'd told me in the beginning, "*Non mi passa!*" ("Don't pass me!"), I thought he was kidding, but I knew now he wasn't. He didn't want the only woman cycling on the trip to cycle faster than he did, and he'd reminded me of it on several occasions.

I tried to adhere to his wishes, but cycling behind him spoiled my natural rhythm and caused me to have to work harder. By now I'd become pretty good at using momentum to help me keep up with them. Going as fast as I could in a descent to get up a good head of steam, I'd milk the momentum for all it was worth as I pedaled like hell up the next hill.

Dottore, instead, sometimes would coast down a hill, slowing almost to a stop at the bottom before starting to pedal up the next hill, so in hilly terrain I'd try to pedal in a different part of the group. I knew he didn't want to be teased by the others, so if I started out with Dottore, I'd try to stay behind him. It was by his okay, I remembered, that I was here.

More and more, I found myself wanting to cycle apart from Nino. I was confused by my changing attitude toward him, this man with whom I was contemplating a future. I loved his company, respected and enjoyed his intellect, had strong feelings for him. But at the same time I was irked by the way he treated me in front of the men. I couldn't figure it out. He'd tell me loudly within earshot of other cyclists what an easy hill it was when it wasn't at all, and he damn well knew it. He'd yell, "Fifty meters to go!" as if I were handicapped. When I'd be puffing up a hill, he'd embarrass me by telling nearby cyclists that I was the "Iron Woman," in spite of my having asked him not to call me that. Or he'd make a show of pushing me as he'd seen Bruno and Umberto do, when he actually wouldn't be pushing me at all.

He continued to tell me negative comments he said one or the other of the men had made about me. He talked to the others about how supportive he was of my cycling on the trip, but it seemed he was trying to sabotage my efforts. *Oh, for cryin' out loud*, I lectured myself, *don't be so paranoid. Maybe my independence grates on him the way his real or imagined condescension irritates me.* I just wanted him to leave me alone so I could do it as I could do it.

Whatever the case, I was happy now to be pedaling between groups, alone, with no one's rhythm to follow but my own. I liked cycling alone at times, to hear the sounds of the earth and the satisfying crunch of my tires on the road.

For now our lives were on the bicycle, on the road. We stretched out through the heart of the Alps. The mountains were big, the climbs long. There was a quiet over the countryside as small clusters of us climbed at our own pace. A peace had settled over us, alone in this country but together as a group, soaking up the spectacular beauty of our surroundings in silent camaraderie.

Occasionally, through the quiet of the countryside, a rich baritone would carry back to me on the wind; Antonio would have burst forth into song. "*O solo mio-o-o...*" I'd smile, loving the Italian feeling of the moment. Suddenly I felt like I was in a movie.

Uh-oh, another town was approaching. I knew this meant we'd speed up to have the desired effect upon the comely young ladies on street corners, watching us go by. Led by Luigi, their machismo in high gear, the men whooped at pretty girls as we swept through. It was like being in the middle of a large, organic, moving male body. At these times I experienced their maleness as one of them, instead of as a woman, and it had the peculiar thrill of forbidden fruit. At the same time, I was ever aware of my femaleness. I felt it reflected in the protectiveness of the men, and I basked in it.

After the town we spread out in several packs again. Nino seemed to prefer cycling in the rear of the group while I liked pedaling in the middle, alone between groups, but they were always reeling me in and pointing at someone for me to draft. It was dawning on me that someone was always keeping a pretty close eye on me, and I could see that there had been some prior agreement about it. The men who took turns riding herd on me didn't include Nino, I noticed. More and more, Nino and I cycled in different parts of the pack.

I was getting pretty good at drafting, which was a necessity now because we were traveling at about eighteen miles per hour. The problem was that I had to keep my eye on the guy I was drafting, or his wheel, rather than the scenery. This was pretty constricting, but on the flat I had to draft to keep up. I was grateful that the men were helping me do it. Like me, they were thrilled to be here, pedaling. You could feel the joy in the group; it was palpable.

Can I Do This?

But the pain never went away, and it wore me down. Would we never get to Salzburg? The muscles in my legs were in constant pain from pushing myself to go faster than my legs could go, trying to spin faster, trying to keep up. Tears of fatigue flowed, blown off my face by the wind under my glasses. I couldn't help it. *God, don't let anybody notice.* Let's face it, these guys really were stronger than I was. I'd known it intellectually; now I knew it in every fiber of my muscles.

Angelo interjected, "*They're not all stronger than you, kid.*"

"Oh yeah?" Though close to my edge, I straightened my back and took a deep breath. I was not one to pass up an opportunity for such a great adventure. Most of the adventurous women I'd read about had their adventures alone, as I'd had many of mine. But I was doing it with them now, and I'd do it until I dropped. Which wasn't far off. I just didn't realize there would be so much pain.

"Hey. They're in pain too."

"Oh. Okay." Not much consolation, though.

At last we entered the fairy-tale city of Salzburg, but I was so done in that all I could think about was getting to the hotel. Never had I been so wiped out after a day of cycling. As we stashed our bikes in the garages behind the hotel, my legs shook so much I had trouble walking, and the chafing between my legs was making me walk gingerly and a little bowlegged. But some of the others were bumping into things and walking funny too; they had their own problems. I found Nino, and we groped our way to our room.

I'd just flopped down on the bed after my shower when Nino informed me we'd have to get passport photos taken here for our Czech visas, which we'd acquire at the border. I was so tired I didn't think I could walk downstairs let alone downtown, but Nino was adamant.

We walked around until we found a place that could do it. I felt awful. I needed tissues and a few other things, but I couldn't face trying to find them, even though this might be the only opportunity; anything I needed paled in importance beside needing to rest. I was lightheaded and weaving. My eyes weren't focusing. Doubts were attacking me like little needles: *How can I keep on doing this? How can I do it tomorrow? What if I really can't make it?* No! How could I face this failure? Okay, I could pick myself up and try again some other time. But *this* opportunity would never come again, never. I could live with the failure of my body, but not with the failure of my will. I'd just pedal till I dropped. I realized now this was more than just a statement of bravado; it was actually a possibility.

I was in trouble, more than just tired. I was even having trouble thinking. I begged Nino to find us a cab, but he never takes cabs and refused to try to find one. I didn't see one, so we walked back to the hotel.

Sitting at last on the bed again, I began to sob with fatigue, losing control of myself completely. I sobbed uncontrollably for a long time.

Nino wrung his hands, not knowing what to do. He said, "Maybe it's time for you to quit."

I screamed at him, "It's not an option! What the hell would you know or care about it? Just go away! Get out! Leave me alone!"

Looking hurt, he went down to dinner alone.

I knew I had to eat, even though I felt miserable and wasn't the least bit hungry. I tried to mop myself up, using Nino's eye drops and putting on a little more blush and lipstick than usual, hoping it would camouflage my fatigue. It didn't. A glimpse in a mirror by the elevator showed a reflection as white as a ghost.

Taking a deep breath as I entered the dining room, I held my head up and smiled at people. I felt as drained and spent as the mirror had reflected, and wished I hadn't seen it. Longing to be less self-conscious, I watched the men watch me. I hated seeing the concern on their faces, and would've given anything to be invisible.

I sat with Nino and Franco, a handsome, blond, Swiss-Italian who strutted and postured a lot. When I sat down Franco looked as if he wanted to escape, making me feel even worse. Nino was sullen, and didn't ask how I was feeling. Glad for once not to participate in the conversation, I forced down some dinner.

After dinner, Nino went with Dottore and the others on a walking tour of Salzburg. Not sorry to miss it, I could hardly wait to go upstairs, grateful for the first time that we had twin beds. I hoped I could keep dinner down.

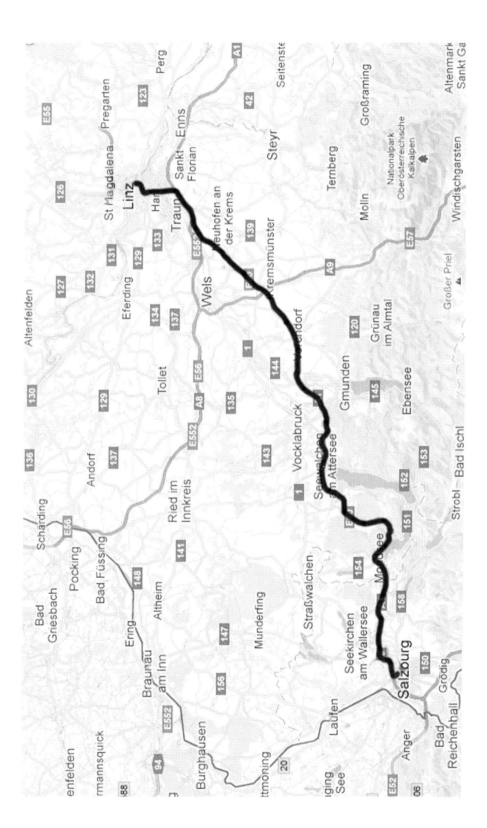

10

Day Four: Salzburg to Linz, 101 Miles

Just Like One of the Boys

I awoke at first light. My first breath caught in my throat, a sob close to the surface. Nino was still asleep. I got up, feeling like I'd been run over by a tank. Nino usually awoke when I did, so I walked softly into the bathroom to be alone. Shutting the door quietly and putting a towel on the floor, I sat down cross-legged to meditate. Every breath caught in a sob in my throat, and it seemed to take a long time to feel calm, centered, grounded. I visualized drawing in energy and strength from God and the universe, from my father, and from Angelo.

Please, God, I prayed, *give me the strength to get through this day, on my bicycle.* With my prayer I realized anew that the totality of my commitment would not allow me to quit, even if I knew I was injuring myself, knew my life was at risk. For the first time I could see the real risk I was taking. A physical pang of fear shot through me, telling me I could lose my life by an action I was taking—a deep, mortal fear, different from being merely afraid. This kind of fear was God's way, I suddenly understood, to warn you of imminent danger.

Quietly, I accepted my commitment and its outcome. My fate was not in my hands alone any longer; it was also in God's.

Nino was up when I emerged from the bathroom. He announced, "You know, you've lost all of your femininity on this trip—you're just like one of the boys," winning the bad timing award for the year. The ludicrousness of his remark might have amused me if I hadn't been dealing with issues of real survival.

I suppressed a surge of rage, wanting to keep the strength I had gathered. Since I couldn't think of anything to say that wouldn't have been an insult and a diffusion of my precious energy, I dressed silently and we went down to breakfast.

I thought about it over my coffee while the caffeine sent its own energy into my veins, glad Nino was busy talking with the others at our table. I realized I was indeed invoking every shred of masculinity within me in order to complete this trip. But was it masculinity? No! Courage and grit are traits of some women, as well as of some men.

But one thing was certain: the qualities that men seek in women were not the qualities that would get me through this trip. The chic woman on Nino's arm strolling down a street in Florence was not the same as the lady with the set jaw pedaling now with the men, even though we both resided in the same body. I could be both of these women, but—I knew now—not at the same time.

What kind of twisted ideas about being a woman do I hold that make me feel split into two women now? Whatever my own thoughts, the split was reinforced by the positive male reaction to the one, and the mostly negative male reaction to the other. *And yet,* I thought into the coffee, *I am not a reflection. I am an existing, independent being, and the chips will have to fall where they fall.* But it was hard. Well, so what? I finished my coffee and went out alone to find my bike.

Standing in the pack straddling our bikes, we waited for Dottore to push off. Still smoldering from our earlier exchange, I turned to Nino and said, "You know, I am more than just my femininity, but still, my femininity is just as precious to me as your stupid balls are to you and I didn't appreciate your remark. In fact, it was the most asinine thing I've ever heard you say."

For the first time, he looked at me with an open and cold dislike. "I don't want to talk to you for the rest of the trip," he announced.

Fine, I thought, *then I won't have to listen to any more assaults on my confidence.* It was becoming clear that the price exacted by my continuing success probably would be my relationship with Nino.

Right then I didn't give a damn.

Unwanted Help

By now I'd picked up a little Italian. Listening to the conversation while we were waiting to start, I recognized the words, *salita lunga* (long hill), *ripida* (steep) and *dura* (hard). The elevation sheet for today showed a sixteen-kilometer climb, with the first three or four the steepest. We all set off behind *Il Capo* Dottore, who led off every day.

No sooner had we turned a corner than there it was. Under ordinary circumstances I'd have known God was not to blame for the climb starting before we'd even digested breakfast or left town, but today I wasn't so sure. Whatever the case, there it was. I gulped, geared down, and started slowly up the grade, which extended steeply for as far as I could see.

Pretty soon most of the cyclists had passed by. Pedaling beside Dottore and commenting on the lovely day, suddenly I started to the shock of the electric hand on my back, hostility pulsing through it as before. The hand radiated not a desire to help, but just-get-this-damn-woman-up-the-hill.

By some prior decision of which I had not been a part, apparently it had been agreed that Luigi would push me up the grade so I wouldn't hold up the group.

I was furious—at him for not being asked if I wanted to be pushed, for needing to be pushed, for not being strong enough to keep up. *Macho bastard*, I thought, *I'll show him. Does he think I can't do it myself?* I had too much pride to disintegrate the way he was obviously sure I would. *He'd like me to give up, get out of his hair, and ride in the van. The hell I will.*

He was pushing me so fast I had to shift up two gears because he was pushing me faster than I could spin the pedals. I gritted my teeth, trying to ignore the burn in my thighs. He adjusted his hand so his middle finger was hooked into the home position in my rear.

Enraged at this overt act of aggression, I yelled at him, "You son of a bitch miserable bastard, get your hand off my butt!" Panting, I looked around to see if he understood.

He was smiling. Even though he spoke no English, he understood, all right, and was enjoying every minute of my rage. *Macho, arrogant bastard!* I was gasping for breath now, gripping the dropped ends of the handlebars, trying to find the right gear so I wouldn't have to spin so fast. I would *not* collapse under this abuse. I'd die first.

He saw my determination, and how much I cared about it, and he let up a little. Every time he pushed me I put my hands on the drops in a sprint position for better leverage, even though we were going uphill. I gasped for breath whenever he pushed me, because I had to work several times as hard as I would going up the hill at my own pace.

He yelled at me in Italian and pantomimed, *don't put your hands on the drops—hands on top, breathe better, breathe the way I do*, as he inhaled mightily and pounded his chest. "*Respira!*" ("Breathe!") he ordered. Each time I reached for the lever to shift into an easier gear, he'd bark, "*Non cambia!*" ("Don't change!") Watching to gauge my effort, he'd order, "*Cambia!*" at the outer edge of my endurance. The hand he was pushing me with moved almost imperceptibly into a slightly less offensive position. His hostility began to dissolve into teaching. He gave me another push. I milked every ounce out of the momentum, reaching for the shift lever at the end of it, only to hear him shout, "*Non cambia!*" again.

This made me push just a little harder beyond what I could do only a kilometer before. It pushed my limits and touched me deep in my soul in a place that changed me forever. At that moment I felt the love for the sport that Luigi felt. *So this is what it is all about. So this is cycling.* I felt as if I discovered, experienced the depth of the sport only at this moment.

Perhaps it was just as well we couldn't talk to each other. This shared passion could easily turn into something else. He didn't look directly at me, nor I at him. It felt dangerous.

I wanted him to tell me his name, even though I knew it, but I couldn't remember how to ask in Italian. "Lina," I said, pointing at myself. "*Non La Americana*, okay?" I hoped he'd understand that I wanted to be thought of as a person, not as a generic American female nuisance. He smiled his understanding with one corner of his mouth. I pointed at him, indicating I wanted to know his name.

"Ugolini," he grunted, not wanting to share the friendliness of his first name.

"No, Lina." I pointed at myself and then at him.

He appeared to relax a little and answered, "Luigi," his voice softening just a bit.

Luigi's background as a top-ranked *corridore* (racer) had made him tough, and hard as nails. Furtively, I'd watched him pacing around in the group. Even though he was probably in his fifties, whenever he encountered an obstacle he'd casually vault over it with an effortless grace, as if he were fifteen. I found myself fascinated by him, and had to force myself not to stare. The aura of his virility reached out far beyond him; I'd felt it like an electric current through his hand on my back.

As he spoke, his tall, lanky frame was draped almost sidesaddle on his bicycle as he pedaled effortlessly beside me up the hill. How in hell does he do that? The grade lessened a little, and I found the right gear. I studied him now at close range. It was like looking a wild animal in the eye. Tall, lean, and wide-shouldered, he carried himself with ease and grace. His graying hair set off his bronze face, hard and set, like a sculpture. Passion seemed to smolder in his deep-set brown eyes. His nose was long and thin, his face all angles. His rare, lopsided smile sent a strange chill up my spine. There was a magnetism about him that made him handsome, made him—I decided not to think about it. He exuded more maleness than any man I'd ever met, passing my "no clothes test" with no trouble at all.

I had a quirky way of looking at men. I'd visualize the man naked—not because I wanted to see him undressed, but because I wanted to see if he needed his clothes as a prop. I could always tell this by picturing him without them. If he didn't need them, then that was a real man, in my book.

Luigi swept an arm toward the scenery, reminding me to see it. He told me something in Italian, I told him something in English, and we laughed at our inability to communicate. We came to the top of the hill, and I raced downhill ahead of him, unabashedly showing off. He chased me down the hill and looked at me with the question in his eyes: *How, for a woman, are you able to do that?* I couldn't tell him about the ski racing, and I was happy to let him wonder, to be as much of a mystery to him as he was to me.

We were in the heart of the Austrian Alps. The mountainsides, under snow-covered granite peaks, were impossibly green. The vast, steep meadows were woven with forests and dotted with chalets and tiny villages presided over by church steeples. A quiet morning mist rose from alpine lakes, softening bright spring colors, capriciously hiding the storybook chalets I strained to see. The mist lent to the landscape an aura of dreamlike surrealism, blurring the lines between real and imagined worlds.

As we approached the rest of the pack, Luigi pedaled off to join his friends. I didn't see Nino—or maybe I didn't want to—so I joined another group of the men. Though unable to talk to them, I still managed to make friends with smiles, gestures, eyes. Many of them were open and friendly, with easy smiles. Now most seemed ready to accept me at whatever level I chose to participate, or perhaps I just hadn't noticed it before. They were doctors, mechanics, bookkeepers, and shoemakers, living their dream and their passion: to be pedaling out on the open road.

Old Luigi's Machismo

The oldest cyclist on the trip, Old Luigi they called him, suddenly fell. He'd been drafting too closely, someone said, and maybe he hadn't reacted fast enough to the rider in front of him. As I pulled over, a group was gathered around him. He was lying on the ground. Francesco, a male nurse cycling with the group, was kneeling beside him, applying a butterfly bandage to the split in his forehead and wrapping a gauze bandage around his head. Old Luigi was shaking and in shock, and the wound was still bleeding through the bandage. Over the protests of Dottore and the group, he got up unsteadily and walked around.

Cycling was what Old Luigi lived for. Now he looked all of his seventy-two years, with a pot belly, slightly spindly but muscular legs, hair a little sparse, but with a fine mustache. He had kind, laughing blue eyes, and always inquired after my welfare. We'd exchanged glances at meals, each knowing what it was costing the other to keep up.

At dinner one night he told me, through Nino, that he'd only begun cycling fifteen years ago, making him fifty-seven when he started. He was a barber, and he cycled every day. He'd been in forty competitions since then, finishing in the top ten for his age group in many of them. The fourth of ten children, he hadn't cycled when he was young because his family was poor. There'd been no money for a bicycle. But as a boy, the cycling legends of the day had been his heroes. I told him what a hard sport I thought cycling was. His face lit up with pleasure as he told me that it wasn't hard for him, because it was his passion. He told me I must have strength of character if

I wanted to succeed as a cyclist, that it was more important than training. "The will drives the body," he said. "Cycling gives me more pleasure than anything in the world."

Now Dottore wanted him to ride in the van. "*No!*" he said. He told Dottore and the group that if they made him ride in the van, he'd turn around and ride home alone on his bicycle. He said he hadn't come all this way to quit and ride in a van, and if he was going to die, he'd do it on his bicycle, not in a van. No amount of cajoling could convince him otherwise.

We watched him start out unsteadily on his bicycle, his kindly, lined face clouded with pain, his jaw set. Lord, what balls. I was learning to respect the machismo my feminism had always made me deride.

For an Italian man, to be macho is to be fully male, fully alive. There were some really tough men on this trip, and I think that if Italians wanted to fight, they'd be among the best fighters in the world. But the national character is not inclined to it. Why fight when there are better and happier choices in life? So the channel for machismo in Italy is sports.

Now I understood why women in Italy didn't appear to have the cultural sanction to participate; most sports in Italy are a closed male club. There are exceptions, but generally girls are shut out at an early age, at the encouragement level and then at the training level. Cycling in Italy is macho and male, with a creed of suffering and glory. The Italians think I'm a real aberration. They didn't know that in California I'd been playing baseball since I was seven or eight, just like many other little girls my age, or that I'd had the bicycle, the freedom, and the will to peddle all over the Oakland hills by myself when I wasn't playing baseball, encouraged by my father. When he told me I could do practically anything if I tried long or hard enough, I bought it completely, even as later sports injuries taught me that this philosophy played a lot easier on the tongue than it did on the ground.

La Simpatia e Morta

Nino caught up with me and we rode together in silence as the rolling hills of the Alps slipped by. The hills were gentle, but we pedaled over hill after hill after hill. I was pushing, trying to do it right, tiring. Where was the rest stop? In spite of my will to hold them back, tears welled up again, blown away by the wind. I bit my lip and pushed harder, realizing that I was facing my own machismo. I didn't want any damn understanding or sympathy from Nino, either. Riding just ahead or behind him, I didn't want him to see me crying. I needed to do this alone, uncluttered and unaffected by any of his other agendas. I knew he was waiting for me to fold.

He appeared to have forgotten our morning disagreement, and his tanned face was full of concern. I knew he wondered if I was all right, and that I didn't want him to ask. *So help me*, I thought, *if he says, "Only fifty yards to go," I'll whack him with my pump.* Even as I formulated the thought, I was sorry for my bitchiness, and knew he didn't deserve it.

Finally he announced, "*La simpatia e morta.*" ("Sympathy is dead.")

I burst out laughing, realizing I was feeling sorry for myself. Nino was a good man; he cared about me, even if he didn't understand me. This was because we were so different; he couldn't know who I really was, because of who he was.

Nino had been an American for forty years. But he grew up an Italian in Italy, with all the attitudes of Italian men of that day toward women: that their place was in the home, over which the man was the supreme authority, and not in the workplace where jobs were more deserved by men. As he'd become successful, he'd been both manager and owner of stock brokerages, and had hired many women as brokers. He was proud of that and spoke of it often, to show his egalitarianism.

At the same time, I heard him make only derogatory remarks about any woman, and a knowing had slowly dawned on me that Nino really didn't like women. It can be hard for a woman to spot a man who doesn't like women, because such men disguise their misogyny with courting for sexual favors.

Nino may not even have realized he was undermining my confidence with his little barbs; I'll never know. Strangely, with all our differences, I liked and respected him. I wouldn't have dreamed of telling him this, because he was already much too conceited and arrogant. He liked and respected me too, but he would have died rather than tell me so, because he thought I was already too willful and opinionated. Aware of it or not, though he was voicing his support for my effort, I felt that in his heart he didn't want me to succeed. Whatever the case, more often than not I stayed away from him while we were cycling because I felt stronger when I cycled with the others.

We pedaled slowly, to rest a little. He offered me a banana, which I gratefully accepted. We took in the sweeping view of rolling farmlands blanketed with new crops and rich green fields. Groves of trees grew by frequent ponds and small lakes. Even though we were far out in the country, farmhouse chalets were tucked in by every pond, and next to groves of trees. There was no wilderness here, as we know it in America. The country was friendly and inviting; it had a safe, hospitable feel. It wasn't big, raw, and empty, or dangerous and unpredictable, like stretches of American wilderness can be.

Fearing I might blame my fatigue on poor Nino since he was handy, I fell back a little before I said anything I'd be sorry for later. We pedaled for what seemed like a long time. I cried into the wind. I wasn't unhappy; I just couldn't help it. It was the fatigue that made me cry, and I had the odd experience of enjoying the scenery as I pedaled and cried.

The gorgeous alpine countryside distracted me from the ever-present pain in my legs. At last we arrived at Bad Ischl, a little jewel of a resort town that looked as if it had been lifted out of a travel poster.

We had come a hundred kilometers (sixty miles) without a rest stop. I slipped quietly behind a bush to pull myself together, until I could breathe without a sob catching in my throat.

Bad Ischl

On my way to the food van, I passed Franco, shaking and crying in the empty garden of a sidewalk café. I walked quietly past so he wouldn't know I'd seen him. He had just bought his bike and hadn't trained for this trip. Now he was paying; only real machismo could make it here.

The talk was we'd stay here for awhile, so I could relax. I wandered around the lovely park, sheltered by weeping willows and the spreading boughs of large shade trees. A festival was going on. There were American flags all over the place. What? Of all things, it was an "America" festival, and many people were in costume, dressed as cowboys, Indians, and pioneer women.

I went up to a group standing by a mock covered wagon with a picture of a buffalo on it and proudly announced, "I'm an American!"

They looked at me strangely, turned their backs, and went back to their German conversation. They were celebrating their fantasy, and wanted no part of the real thing.

I've learned from my roaming about the world that one frequently encounters situations for which there is absolutely no explanation, nor will you ever get one. This was one.

Wandering back to my Italian friends, I felt oddly as if I were returning home. One of Dottore's favorite polkas was playing from one of the vans, and he was whirling Luciana joyously around the parking lot to the applause of admiring onlookers. Taking my place in the *panino* line, I noticed more enthusiasm than usual at the prospect of lunch. What was that white stuff being sliced? Nino, who had come up behind me, read my mind and said, "Lard sandwiches."

Oh dear God, no! How am I going to pedal for the rest of the day on a lard sandwich? How am I going to *eat* a lard sandwich? The men were overjoyed, munching lustily, regarding this a rare treat. I decided to pretend it was bacon-flavored tofu. I tried; I really did. Couldn't do it.

I looked imploringly at Nino, who kindly found me some cheese for my bread. I sighed; a picture popped into my head of a fresh turkey on whole-wheat sandwich, laden with lettuce, tomatoes, and mayo—salt and pepper, maybe a little cranberry sauce. Americans have the sandwich genes. As I gnawed on my better-than-lard-but-no-gourmet-repast dry *panino*, I was rescued by Luciana, Maria Pia, and several other of the wives, who invited me to join them for a pastry in the town.

The shopping area of Bad Ischl was shaded by large, old plane trees. The streets and sidewalks had a fresh-scrubbed look, and the old buildings looked freshly painted. Many were a soft yellow with white trim, giving the lovely town a festive air. The windows of the pastry shop were filled with mouthwatering little works of Bavarian art masquerading as pastry, exquisitely crafted.

Inside, small round tables were of richly grained marble, with chairs of gilt and brocade upholstery. Clouds and cherubs were painted on arched ceilings.

I became suddenly aware that someone didn't smell very good. Oh God, it was me. My jersey was stained with sweat, never mind my tights and sweat-matted hair. The other ladies were impeccably attired in dresses, and smelled like they should. But they seemed glad to have me, so I relaxed. As they laughed and talked, I caught the names of their husbands. They were making fun of the men! I *hated* not being able to join them in this. They were bursting with curiosity about my relationship with Nino, and Luciana attempted to ask me how it was going. With my meager Italian and some pantomime, I rolled my eyes and tried to convey that sometimes it went well, sometimes it didn't, and that Nino wasn't too crazy about Lina the cyclist. They understood perfectly, and we had a good laugh. At that moment I vowed to learn Italian and return someday, and then we could *really* have a good laugh.

After lunch, local people in the park came over to inquire who we were and where we were going, although by now someone had made a huge sign and mounted it on one of the vans saying, "Verona—Stans—Praga—Varsavia." I don't know what effect it had on the townspeople, but it sure as hell impressed me. As we shared our wine with them, their looks of amusement betrayed their impression that we were one big traveling party—which wasn't far from the truth.

Bruno

I spotted Bruno sitting by himself on a wall, eating his *panino*. He often kept to himself. He caught my eye and smiled, so I ambled over to join him. Bruno was a highly skilled cyclist, but didn't look the part. He was slight and graying, with soft, kind blue eyes and a gentle demeanor. Quiet and shy, he had the air of a cultured man. He was the only one of the group who knew a little English. I'd drafted him from time to time, because he was a consistent, smooth cyclist and because he'd invited me. Now he told me more about his family.

His mother was Italian but his father had been a well-known French bicycle racer before the war. He'd trained Bruno, hoping he would follow in his footsteps. But it was early in the 1940s, and his father, like other fathers, had gone off to war, and would not come home. Bruno knew he didn't have the competitive edge, the aggressive instinct, to become a professional racer. Although he missed his father sorely, he was glad to be freed from following in what he knew would be the wrong footsteps. Now he cycled only for the joy of it—never to compete.

He was married and had three grown children and five grandchildren, but he spoke most often about his unmarried daughter. His eyes clouded over and he wrung his hands in worry as he told me that, at age thirty, she'd moved out of the family home into her own apartment. In Italy it is only now beginning to be acceptable for an unmarried woman to have her own apartment. His worry was not appeased by my telling him this was a normal event in America.

He asked many questions about life in California, and we stumbled through our conversation with our small vocabulary of mutually understood words. Finally we just sat together silently on the wall enjoying the warm sun on our backs, content with the intention of our friendship.

The Privacy Issue

The remaining forty miles went by quickly. We wound through the valleys, following the flat terrain. The pedaling was easy, allowing all of us to enjoy the countryside, dotted with geraniumed chalets climbing up green mountainsides.

Suddenly I had to relieve myself. The group I was pedaling with had made a stop for this purpose a little while ago. Modesty prevented me from joining them, even with the privacy of my very own bush, hooray. Usually I'd try to cycle ahead a little, or wait until I was pedaling alone between groups to drop my bicycle, grab my tissues and dash for the bushes, after which I'd have to pedal like hell to catch up. If I took too long someone would come back to look for me, having spotted my bicycle beside the road. They'd stop and call loudly, "*C'e problema, Lina?*"

Oh jeez.

Today I was pedaling between groups. I stopped and made my way into the bushes, wondering if there was any scientific basis for the psychological obstinacy of the human elimination system, tied in knots in the presence of luxurious bathrooms, but incapable of waiting when there were none. Holding the tissue package in my teeth as I struggled with bicycle tights and thorns on bushes, I remembered past difficulties—while wearing a jumpsuit, pantyhose, and a shoulder bag— negotiating the squat toilets still found in nice restaurants in rural France and Italy. Compared to that, the bushes were a breeze.

Stuck on the Autobahn

As we approached Linz, we passed a sign proclaiming a population of three hundred thousand. Linz came complete with freeways. The plan was that one of the vans would lead us through the city. The problem was that, as usual, none of them had been here before.

Dutifully following our designated navigator, we suddenly found ourselves, all fifty-four of us, marooned on the median strip of an eight-lane autobahn in the middle of rush-hour traffic. What the hell…? We all looked around, and at each other. How could this possibly have happened? No one knew. Also, no one knew what to do. Some of the riders laughed sheepishly, some looked embarrassed, and Antonio slapped his forehead and proclaimed, "*Dio mio!*" Everyone had something to say about it, and all of us talked at once and waved our arms, as usual.

Finally we straggled over to the side of the freeway a few at a time, to the honking of horns, blasphemous remarks in German from drivers waving fists out of car windows, and the backing up of traffic. There were, after all, fifty-four of us, and we still didn't know what to do. Dottore was making things worse by stopping cars and conversing through windows about where we should go.

Pretty soon we heard sirens in the distance. We cringed and rolled our eyes, knowing they were for us. The police arrived in four cars, lights flashing and whirling, sirens blaring. The policemen, wearing riot gear (maybe they thought we were aliens, which, I suppose would have been more interesting than just a huge bunch of Italian screw-ups on bicycles), stalked about in full face helmets and tall leather boots, looking (down) at us, shaking their heads and saying incredulously, "You are on the autobahn! This is the rush hour!" (We'd noticed.)

The good Dottore, who spoke German, tried unsuccessfully to

appease them. They told him they'd escort us to our hotel, as well as out of town in the morning, so we wouldn't be "a menace to the city." Humph. I suppose *they* never made a little mistake.

This at least gave them an excuse to rail at Italians, the favorite inter-ethnic sport in Europe. (Northern Europeans feel superior to and envy Italians; Italians from the north look down upon Italians from the south, who poke fun at Germans, who don't like the French, who hate the Germans and lose their ability to speak coherently if you mention the word, "Algerian"; and everybody hates gypsies, thinks Russians are strange, and criticizes and envies Americans.)

We were off the freeway at last, but the hazards didn't end there. The streets were wet from a recent rain and were full of trolley tracks—a cyclist's urban nightmare. If you have to cross them you must do so as perpendicularly as possible to prevent your wheel (all of us rode skinny-tired racing bikes) from getting caught between the wet, slippery metal rail and the pavement or cobblestones.

Suddenly I found myself squeezed out of room to ride between the tracks and the curb, and I jerked my bike over into the middle of the tracks. There was never time for all of us to make it through a green light, so the rest of us went through red lights in order not to lose the group, avoiding startled pedestrians and cars entering the intersection from cross-streets.

This would be no trick for a San Francisco bike messenger, but the three miles to our hotel were a death-defying journey for me, bringing up the rear with the stragglers. At one point I almost ran into a woman in a crosswalk trying to avoid snagging the leash between her and her dog. There was some comfort in knowing the locals would blame it all on the Italians, and that as long as I kept my mouth shut I wouldn't have to take the rap as an American, for a change.

Thank You for Your Lousy Service

Arriving at the hotel, we made our entrance behind the police with a great flourish to a large audience of applauding sidewalk café patrons. We enjoyed the fun and basked in the attention for a few minutes until an argument ensued over security for our bicycles, which the hotel thought would be all right parked outside all night. Many of these guys valued their bicycles more than their cars. The paint jobs were incredibly ornate on the Chesinis, the De Rosas and others, all expensive. No way were those bikes going to sit outside all night. Finally the hotel relented, and we were grudgingly given an empty banquet room to store our bikes.

As usual, it took me an hour to scrub off the road grime, do the laundry, wash my hair, and dress. Every night I had to wash my cycling clothes, since even if the hotel had a laundry service, they could never get it done by the next morning. I'd brought three pair of cycling shorts: one to wear, one drying or waiting to be washed, and one clean.

I had a system, which I taught Nino. Throwing my day's cycling clothes into the shower with me, I'd soap them up with the bar of Italian laundry soap I'd brought. Then I'd gently stomp on them while I bathed, so they'd be almost rinsed when I was. After wringing them out by hand, I'd roll them up flat in a dry towel, and walk on the roll for a few minutes. Thus squeezed, they'd almost always be dry by morning. I called it "the hotel laundry stomp."

The Italians, I noticed, addressed this problem by bringing huge duffels with enough changes for the whole trip. How thrilled the little woman at home would be to deal with *this*.

Our overly elegant hotel was large, square, and new, with nice rooms, staff who turned up their noses at cyclists, and overly small portions at dinner in a well-appointed dining room served by snooty waiters.

Our hotels had been booked by a travel agency in Verona. It obviously hadn't been mentioned that cyclists eat much more than normal people. As a result, each table of six cyclists consumed about six baskets of bread in addition to the rest of the food in order to get enough to eat at dinner. When the food arrived, the men pined visibly for a decent plate of pasta. They'd look at each other and roll their eyes at the potatoes and *weinerschnitzel*—comrades-in-suffering. I heard descriptions of the food that contained words I was glad I couldn't understand.

By now I could get off an occasional one-liner in Italian. "*Carne di mistero*" ("mystery meat"), I opined. They chuckled, not used to a wisecracking woman, especially one who got adjectives and things backward.

Dottore announced he'd take anyone who was still ambulatory (count me out) on a walking tour of the town after dinner, and to see the town's cathedral.

Our resident communist, Riccardo, stood up. Arms flailing, he bellowed that he didn't want to see any damn church with silver and gold altars when people in the Third World were starving. Eight or so men bellowed back at him, some came to Riccardo's defense, and more got into the melee. The concierge came in wringing his hands and pleading with us to be quiet, but no one heard him above the din.

Antonio came over and asked Nino to explain to me that this was normal, that they were really all friends. Fists were shaking and the room was reverberating as the cacophony of lustily arguing Italians bounced off the walls. I sipped my wine, reflecting upon the power in any given pair of male Italian lungs. God, it was fun. Nino sat back, enjoying the whole thing. He explained, "Don't worry; in Italy, you're either a Catholic or a communist, and you don't take either one very seriously." I checked to see if he was kidding, but he wasn't.

Finally Riccardo and friends retired to the bar, and Dottore and friends went off to see the church.

The Chasm Grows

Back in our room, Nino remarked about how I'd been short with him earlier in the day. Sitting cross-legged on the bed, I tried to make him understand. "Look, to get through this trip, I have to be a different part of myself than the one that just happily follows you around Florence. I can't play both of these roles at the same time. And it upsets and demeans me when you say, 'Only fifty yards to go to the top of the hill,' because you're addressing my weakness, not my strength. I'm here as a cyclist, not someone in your charge. If you want to help me," I told him, "just be there for me, give me room to grow, tell me only the positive things, and cheer me on silently, in your heart."

He looked at me, trying to understand. I realized then that he simply couldn't.

I was also suddenly aware of my own naïveté in expecting Nino to be able to see who I really was, free of his own notions of what a woman was—or was not.

Accepting others at face value, regardless of their history, was a uniquely American trait—sort of a national naïveté. We're famous, after all, for casting aside history and starting anew. I'd been raised with the notion that people honestly wanted to know each other, that this was possible, and that erroneous preconceptions could be set aright. I clung to these notions, wanting them to be so, like a stubborn bulldog. If I didn't hang on to my notions of the possibilities in life, then how could I go on believing I could complete this trip?

11

DAY FIVE: INTO CZECHOSLOVAKIA
LINZ TO CESKE BUDEJOVICE, 66 MILES

Gender Problems

Dawn found me renewed. *I can do this*. Closing my eyes, I focused on shutting out the fatigue and gathering my energy, storing it up for the day.

The night before, as we were putting away our bicycles, Luigi came over and asked Nino to translate for me that I was doing well, and to keep it up. His acknowledgment gave me new confidence. He said we were out of the Austrian Alps now, and tomorrow we'd cross into Eastern Europe at the Czechoslovakian border. I was glad he'd taken the trouble to come over and tell us this; I wondered if he suspected I wasn't getting the information I needed from Nino (cyclists need to know the mileage and nature of the terrain ahead so they can pace themselves throughout the day).

Nino awoke in an upbeat mood, and we talked about how good we felt that day. As we walked down the hotel corridor toward the elevator on our way to breakfast, I threw my arm around his shoulders and gave him a squeeze. Our friendship was growing, in spite of our problems.

Nino was a thoughtful man, not given to blurting out his opinion at the drop of a hat, like I was. However, his conflicting emotions showed on his face. He loved me, but he wasn't sure if he liked me. He wanted me to succeed, and he didn't. He was critical of me, and proud of me. His probably unconscious underlying assumption that I found so stinging, as a cyclist, was that the woman is less than the man.

I was sorry to have put him through such a hard time with this other part of Lynne, now called Lina, and glad, because I thought he deserved it. But we were friends, after all, even though his negative remarks had taken their toll. I cared deeply about him—did I love him?—I'd thought so, but now I wasn't so sure. In spite of myself, I always had one eye on Luigi.

The subject of sex had come up, but we'd just groan with fatigue, laugh, and fall immediately asleep. But it was more than that. My desire had declined along with my trust.

The War Hero

Nino was tired too. I wasn't the only one pushing my limits. If Nino was suffering, no one would ever know, because that's the way he was. I guess when you're a man who has fought through and survived a world war, you measure every event thereafter with a different yardstick, and tend to think that if something isn't life-threatening, it isn't worth getting too excited about.

Near the end of the war, Nino fought in the trenches in the freezing cold of a Russian winter. In the heat of a battle, he'd walked out of the fighting zone in search of a Red Cross ambulance for his wounded comrades. Finding himself caught behind enemy lines, he'd been unable to return to his men. He walked many miles before he was found and taken to a hospital, where he nearly lost his feet to frostbite. The hospital had patched him up and shipped him home to Italy, where he spent more time in a hospital recovering from severe malnutrition. "God, they—we—were all so young; so many died, so very young," he told me one night over dinner, a shadow of pain crossing his face. "I remember their faces—they haunt me still."

Nino had a beautiful singing voice. He used to tell me how, as a boy in his village in the mountains of northern Italy, people would huddle in the village café in the cold winters and listen to opera on the radio. He remembered the intensity of their listening, and the steam rising from cups of espresso, and how good it all smelled. The village opera connoisseurs would sit at the rickety tables and critique the performances, listening with trained ears to the great singers of the day. In this way he learned the popular arias, and he would sing all the time.

Nino

And he sang in the trenches in Russia, in the cold and the mud. A platoon leader, he led his men crawling through the mud in the trenches, bullets zinging over their heads. Next to Nino, a young comrade raised his head to see what lay ahead, and it was shot off.

Through their agony the others said, "Sing, Nino, sing." And he did, to keep their spirits alive.

He returned home a hero, one of only thirty-seven that survived out of the thousand and fifty young men sent to fight in Russia. After spending time in the hospital rebuilding his war-ravaged body, he returned to his hungry village and its impoverished people. He smuggled food to his village for a time, making runs at night in a horse-drawn wagon, at constant risk of arrest. Nino was strong inside and out, and even now in his sixties, a hill on a bicycle did not intimidate him. No matter how angry with him I became, I always respected him, and his history.

Life on the Road

At breakfast the men were decked out in their cycling finery, as usual. Breakfasts in Austria were wonderful: the tables were covered with platters of delicious, freshly baked breads and rolls, meats and cheeses, cereals, yogurts, fruits, and juices. The problem was that I was never hungry that early. I'd just look at my filled plate, wanting to want it. But I'd learned to stuff it down anyway, since you have to fuel up to cycle the distances. Able to force down only so much, I'd make a sandwich out of what I couldn't eat to stick in my back pocket for later. I'd finally learned to eat while I was pedaling, trying not to squeeze it into an indistinguishable mass and taking bites on the downhill side of rises, sort of like a human fuel-injection system.

Getting out of Linz seemed a simple enough chore. We got an early start, to much joking around, recalling our grand escorted entrance into town by the police, sirens blaring, lights whirling, brakes screeching, heads turning; nothing could have pleased the Italians more. Soon we were off through downtown Linz, following our police escort. They left us only too gladly on the outskirts of the city, admonishing Dottore please not to return with his reckless and irresponsible gang of Italians. There was even more joking around about how we could possibly find our way from here without a police escort.

How, indeed?

No sooner had the police left us and we'd traversed the last out-skirts of the city, than Dottore made a right turn at a sign pointing toward the Czechoslovakian border.

Suddenly we found ourselves on the autobahn. Again. I caught a sideways glimpse of Dottore sucking in his breath between clenched teeth, but with characteristic aplomb and avoiding eye contact with any of us, he simply stopped, turned around and cycled back down the freeway ramp, going the wrong way, as if that's what he'd intended to do all along. We all looked at each other helplessly and followed suit, facing bug-eyed fright on drivers' faces as they accelerated up the freeway ramp only to meet fifty-four Italian cyclists coming the other way. Cyclists don't have enough sense ever to be terrified, so everybody took it in their stride as just another joke of the morning.

Finally headed in the right direction, we stretched out on the road. The terrain evened out, with green, rolling countryside stretch-ing ahead of us as far as the eye could see. When you're on a bicycle, there is no such thing as flat. There is gently rolling and severely rolling, but never flat. The farmlands rolled by as the city melted into the countryside. The skies were gray and quiet, and we had a little rain. The world seems endless in such a place, with no beginning and no end.

Finding my pace and rhythm, I used momentum as much as I could to get up the rollers. By now I had favorites I liked to draft: those who were smooth riders and whom I felt were my friends. I'd learned the names of those I'd ridden with, and now I could recognize most of them by their legs. For a woman who enjoys watching a good pair of male legs, which I unabashedly did, this was indeed paradise.

Here comes Bruno. He was easy to spot because he always wore yellow or orange fluorescent socks, and I'd come to recognize his spin. We chatted a little and he asked, "*Va bene?*"

"*Molto bene*" ("Very well"), I answered. "*Avanti*" ("Go ahead"), I told him.

Then Domenico pulled up beside me. He wore serious glasses and looked like the bookkeeper he was, but out here on the road there was something different about him: a fierce love in his eyes of the freedom we were experiencing, the strength and grace of his body as he rode, in harmony with his endeavor and the earth. A flick of his head invited me to get on his wheel. Matching his cadence, I hung on for as long as I could. As we flew down the road, I imagined he was Peter Pan and we were flying through the sky. Finally he was just a little too fast, and I let him go.

Here comes Dino. No words were spoken. Pedaling up alongside, he carefully checked me over to see that everything was okay. Dino sat with us at dinner almost every night. Unlike some of the others who had multifaceted lives, Dino's whole life was cycling. Now retired, he built all of his own bicycles. He'd been racing since he was thirteen, and lived for little else. Last night at dinner he told us a story of how Italian bicycle racing was in the old days.

Nino translated. "We'd race all morning until we got hungry," Dino told us. "Then we'd stop at an inn for lunch. Everyone would mark their place, where they were in the peloton (pack). After a couple of hours for a good lunch, maybe with a little wine, everyone would return to his marked place, and the race would continue for the rest of the day." We'd laughed, talking about the frenzied way racers had to eat in the big races today; barely slowing down, they grab a "feed bag" from a designated person at a "feeding station" and eat as they cruise in the pack—a metaphor, I thought, for a world becoming a more hurried and less civilized place.

The sky was gray, quiet, and dull. Nino checked in every now and then as the green farmlands glided past. We spread out on the almost empty road. Someone always rode herd on me. We were a moving, organic little piece of Italy. There was only the road, the motion, and us. The hours slipped by. It rained, and it stopped. We talked very little.

Border Between Worlds

When we arrived at the Czechoslovakian border, we stopped for a snack. Luciana took our passports to the Czech soldiers who served as guards at the border-crossing booths. They were overcome with curiosity about our bicycles and came over, a few at a time, to inspect—ogle would be a better word—our bikes. Oreste offered them wine. They refused, looking at it longingly, remembering they were on duty. They retreated to continue their inspection of us through the dingy windows of the border station.

Nino and I went inside to get our visas. I was dismayed to find that the Czech border guards addressed me when I was with Nino in the same way the Italians did. That is to say, not at all. I'd come to think of this as "Italian couple-think." When I wasn't with Nino, they'd address me normally as an individual, one on one. When I was with Nino, they'd address him only. Even when I'd ask a question, they'd answer it to Nino.

One of the guards said in English to Nino, "Do you have her photos for the visa? Where is her passport?" I wanted to take his face in my hand, turn it toward mine and say, "Hey, talk to me, I am *here.*" Instead I said, "I have my photos, my passport is in the pile with the others, and I, too, speak English." Nino gave me a look. *Go soak your head*, I thought.

We emerged with our visas to the usual commotion that followed us wherever we went, as the men horsed around and the border guards tried to count us and our passports, which was impossible because we never stood still.

I pretended not to notice Luigi circling around me, like an animal stalking his prey. He made me so damn nervous I tripped over my own feet and dropped my apple. Whenever I got within ten feet of him I tended to drop things, and I wouldn't let myself look directly at him for fear my interest would show. He had no fear of looking at me; I could feel his eyes burning into me, probing. I never knew a man who made me so nervous.

Just then Ciccio sneaked up behind me and gave me a big hug and a kiss. The men thought this was a great joke, since Nino was right in front of me with his back turned and didn't see the episode. Laughing helplessly, I enjoyed the joke as much as they did.

Dottore was holding forth, and Nino translated. "This is a great moment in history to be crossing this border, because it's the end of communism in Europe. Our dream of a united Europe may extend this far, someday." Only this year had the border opened, freeing travel into Czechoslovakia.

The border guards finally gave up trying to match us to our passports, threw up their hands in defeat, and gave Luciana permission for us to cross.

As we pedaled into eastern Europe, signs of Czechoslovakia's long isolation from the West were everywhere. A dreariness seemed to come over the landscape, more than the intermittent rain. Not fifty meters from the border was a farm, its house unpainted, the barn door hanging from one rusty hinge. The fence had been repaired haphazardly with whatever was at hand: scraps of wood, discarded parts of machinery, old wire. A couple of fields lay fallow. Even the crops drooped. Discouragement was written across the land. The contrast with orderly, prosperous, freshly painted Austria was like a bucket of cold water in the face.

We pedaled across the plains for a long time; it probably seemed longer than it was because the country didn't change much. As we pedaled through a small village, the cobblestone streets slowed us down. The main street was all but deserted. We fell quiet as our wheels bounced over the wet cobblestones. Cold road water thrown up in our faces by our wheels punctuated the impression of cycling into a time-warp where nothing had been fixed, painted, or updated in half a century.

Shop windows on the main street were almost empty, containing only a few items: a couple of plain dresses, a coat, a chair, a few food-stuffs. Young people hung out aimlessly in the small central square by a fountain with no water in it. Tall and lanky, they were mostly blond and unsmiling. They looked undernourished, and they had a furtive air about them. But when they saw us their demeanor changed completely: they waved, they stomped, they screamed, they laughed. You'd think they'd never seen a pack of cyclists before. Well, maybe they hadn't. After all, the border had opened only this year. We waved back, shouting greetings, our own enthusiasm renewed.

Once again out in the country, Aurelio said, "*Pochi paese.*" ("Little of everything country.") There was very little traffic—an occasional Skoda, a few trucks belching black smoke. I tried to hold my breath as I pedaled through the fumes. It rained intermittently.

Being so close to life on the ground on my bicycle, looking in kitchen and parlor windows as I passed, I saw and felt the fabric of people's lives. I rejoiced in the smell of the fresh bread they'd soon eat, and I shivered in the tattered long underwear on clotheslines they'd wear in the winter.

As I peered over fences into people's gardens, I decided that the flower was one of God's greatest gifts to the world. No matter how poor people were or how miserable their lives, they made flowers grow. Gorgeous flowers. You couldn't socialize a flower. You couldn't saturate it with propaganda. You couldn't conquer it with a tank. Squash it and it would grow again. There was nothing you could do to ruin a flower, silent testimony to the triumph of the human spirit. On the road, their beauty fed my soul.

We pedaled through vast fields planted in feed crops, but I saw no animals. Immersing myself in the countryside distracted me from water seeping down into my socks and down the back of my neck. Push, slosh, pull; push, slosh, pull. Rays of sunlight filtered with mist poked tentatively through the dark clouds. We fell into a long pace-line, each rider following the rider in front close enough to draft. It hypnotized me; our cadences unconsciously synchronized, and I could swear our pulses did too. We moved as a single body, quietly, rhythmically.

Horsing around at the Czechoslovakian border

Amore or Nothing

I drafted Dino for as long as I could, and then I decided to drop off and pedal alone since the pace was too fast for me to sustain. We were on the only road to Ceske Budejovice and some of the men were behind me, so I wasn't worried about getting lost. How wonderful to pedal at my own pace! What a relief to not have to keep up for awhile, so I could enjoy the scenery.

When Nino caught up with me I was enjoying myself thoroughly, in spite of the rain. We pedaled along in silence for awhile, but he picked up the pace. It was too early in the day for me to be tired, but I was anyway. I had never fully recovered from the day into Salzburg, even though I'd barred it from my mind—and my saddle sores were getting a little worse every day. They were very painful and could only be eased by days off the bicycle, which I wasn't going to get. "Please, Nino, I've got to stop. I just need to get off my bike seat for one minute; then we can go again." Dismounting my bike with all the agility of a dinosaur, I breathed, "Ahhhhh."

To our surprise, the repair van pulled up behind us. The driver leaped out and grabbed my bike, intending to put it in the van.

"Wait! No!" I yelled, grabbing the other end of my bike. With this tug of war going on, I glanced into the van and saw another rider (whose bike was obviously disabled) holding his hands up to me in mock prayer, with an imploring look. He wanted my bike. "*No way, Jose!*" I yelled, yanking my bike back out of the driver's grasp. "What I really need," I told him, "is *un pezzo di cioccolata e un abbraccio*" ("a piece of chocolate and a hug").

In Italy they don't have the concept of the friendly hug, like we do in California. It's *amore*, or nothing. With a horrified look on his face, the driver said, "*Amore? Amore!?*" I could see he was picturing being forced by some Italian code of chivalry to lie down beside the road with this none-too-young, mud-splattered American woman, and he was clearly aghast at the prospect. He nervously produced a piece of chocolate.

I grabbed it, saying, "*Non amore! Abbraccio! Solo abbraccio!*" ("Not love! A hug! Only a hug!") Oh God, there was no way to explain.

Nino said, "Will you just shut up and get back on your bike so we can get the hell out of here?"

I did, and we did.

As I eased my derriere back onto the saddle, it hurt so bad, in so many places, that try as I might to choke it back, I started to cry again. Almost beside myself with pain, I stood on the pedals every minute or two seeking relief, but my feet hurt almost as much as my rear.

Nino said, "Are you sure you don't want to get in the van?"

One of my favorite pictures popped into my head of pounding him into the ground with a frying pan, like a nail. *Whang! Whang!*

Sliding my glasses down my nose, I gave him a look that would've withered the Eiffel Tower.

"Okay, okay! Just trying to help."

I guess he was, I reluctantly conceded. "How about singing me a song?"

He burst forth with one of his favorite Italian arias. His clear tenor filled the air, and his face lit up with the music. I felt better instantly. He sang so beautifully; my heart filled with love for him at that moment, this infuriating man. Where had he hidden this version of himself during his business years? How happy he was when he spoke his native Italian, and how somber he was when he spoke English; he was truly a different person when he spoke each language.

I wished he'd ask me to sing sometime. I'd sung for Nino at first on our bicycles at home, but he never commented about it so I'd stopped doing it. I wasn't sure he ever noticed, and it fed my suspicion that he was hard of hearing.

But now I appreciated the distraction of his singing; the pain was becoming almost unbearable, from both the saddle sores and the chafing. Fat lot of good the stupid Bag Balm did.

Bag Balm is a Vaseline-like substance that comes in a square green tin with a picture of a contented cow on the top. Really. It is for farmers to use on cows' udders for easier milking—benefitting, I assume, both the cow and the farmer. It has become legendary among American cyclists, not surprisingly from the Midwest, for assuaging chafing in the nether parts from too many hours in the saddle. Edges of underpants can destroy you, so they are not worn with cycling shorts, which are lined with chamois-like materials for comfort and padding. However, it is almost impossible to wash Bag Balm out of chamois; Bag Balm, once applied, is impervious to everything. If infection from saddle sores or chafing occurs, you have had it. All you can do is wear clean shorts every day, use soap and water and medicated powder whenever possible, and pray. And don't dwell on the combination of Bag Balm and medicated powder.

If I can cycle through this I can cycle through anything, I thought, looking for extra strength in the idea, not finding any. Every pedal stroke now was a triumph. I desperately searched for more things to distract me, to make me able to keep doing it. I tried to sing to myself, but I needed my breath. I visualized a barrier between the pain and my remaining strength. I counted the broken lines down the center of the road. I counted the trees. I thought about the "old lady story."

The Old Lady Story

Divorced in my mid-twenties, I decided to follow my childhood dream of becoming a professional singer. Folk singing was the popular music of the day. I found a guitar teacher and cajoled one of the best singing teachers in California into taking me on. I forced myself to practice two hours every day while sitting on a stool facing a sink full of dirty dishes (behavior modification for my compulsive cleaning habits). I told the kids not to interrupt me at these times unless they were actually bleeding. After some struggling early performances, I played regularly in supper clubs and big hotels, my success increasing with my experience.

When I started out as a folk singer in the late sixties, one of my first public performances and most spectacular early flops was at an open-mike night at a dive called the Coffee Gallery in San Francisco's North Beach. The folks who hung out there had been around the block and then some, and so had the club. The burnished wood of the bar shone through the low lights, and the old wood floors creaked. The show room in back was painted black. A spotlight shone blue on the stage through layers of sweet smoke. You could get stoned just sitting there breathing, and you'd never want to see the place during the day.

Scared to death and feeling like a fish out of water, I threaded my way to the stage through long-haired, tie-dyed beats and wannabe poets in Salvation Army jeans. I was ill-prepared for San Francisco's urban coffeehouse culture, having come from an insulated, well-to-do background where people were always polite to each other no matter how they felt.

Perched on a rickety stool in my long red and black cocktail dress, I began to sing my most beautiful song, Leonard Cohen's "Suzanne." They hardly swooned at my performance. I sang on, thinking if they would just listen surely they'd recognize the beautiful song and my wonderful talent. Just then a huge black guy in the front row stood up and yelled, "Hey baby, let's fuck!" I froze in mid-note. The room fell silent, the moment suspended in time. I felt the heat of humiliation rise, and prayed the stage would open up and swallow me. After the long moment of silence, the small room erupted into guffaws. One guy actually rolled on the floor, howling with laughter. Sweat dripping through my mascara under the spotlight, I slid off the stool and put my guitar in its case with as much dignity as I could muster. Looking neither to the right or the left, I stepped down from the stage and made my way down the center aisle and out the door. They were still laughing.

But that's not the story.

The story is what happened when I had to go back there to sing another night, since the place was one of the few around where I could get performing experience. I got as far as the door, when my courage deserted me. I froze there on the sidewalk, clutching my guitar case. I asked the Universe: *What will give me the courage to go back in there?*

Suddenly there was the gift of a vision.

I saw myself as an old lady, sitting on a porch in a rocking chair. The active part of my life was over. As I rocked, looking out to a green meadow, I contemplated my life. What, I asked myself, had I really valued about my life? That I participated! came the resounding reply. That I always had the courage to try, to participate fully, no matter what the results. Now I could see that the results weren't the mark of me as a person. It was my intention, and the trying. I took a deep breath and went in.

Taking a deep pull from my water bottle brought me back to the present, and I remembered the strength that vision had given me over the years. I had a silent conversation with Angelo. "You're going to help me get there, aren't you?"

"*No, you are going to help you get there yourself,*" he answered.

"So can't you do anything about this pain?"

"*No. Just hang in there a little longer, kid; you'll be there soon.*"

"Oh. Okay." I never did tell Nino about Angelo.

It was late afternoon. Where was this town, anyway? Finally we could see a town's outline in the distance—that must be it!

I Make It Again

There was only one large building besides the church in the town. We pedaled toward it, figuring this must be the hotel. It was a picturesque town, in an urban, old-world sort of way. Traffic was light; I guessed not many private cars were owned here.

The jarring as our bikes bumped over the cobblestone streets in the commercial center shot pain through me anew. At the hotel at last, Nino seemed none the worse for wear, but I was barely able to get off my bike. My nose ran, my bladder ran, my tears ran.

My knees buckled as I got off my bike, and my bike and I fell in a heap just outside the walled garden of the hotel. I was glad Nino had gone in ahead, and no one saw me. I tried to get up, but I couldn't. Sitting on the sidewalk curb with my feet in the gutter, I sobbed uncontrollably. With the aid of a telephone pole at the edge of the sidewalk, I pulled myself to my knees and finally to my feet. I couldn't stop sobbing as I clung to it for support.

Sensing someone there, I turned in surprise to find Luigi. Brows knit in concern, his eyes searched my face. He put one hand on my shoulder and the other, in a fist, on my heart. His quiet voice urgent and intense, he said, "*Forza, Lina*" ("Be strong, Lina"). Taking a deep breath, I closed my eyes, summoning up my last shreds of stamina and control. I opened my eyes to see respect in his; they were telling me, *Don't fold now—you can do it.* My instinct told me he wanted me to be proud of who I was, as he was proud, and not to let the others see my pain. He squeezed my shoulders and shook me a little; I knew he was trying to send me some strength. Then he went back inside.

Townspeople passed by, looking at me curiously. Finally I squared my shoulders, took a deep breath, and went in.

In the hotel lobby, everyone searched my face and asked, concern on their faces, "*Va bene, Lina?*"

"*Va bene, va bene,*" I lied, finding a smile through bloodshot eyes, runny nose, dirt-streaked face, wobbly legs, raw crotch, saddle sores, numb hands, and feet I could hardly walk on. *Hey, what do you know, I made it again.* My body was a wreck, but my spirit soared. I was here, wasn't I?

Ceske Budejovice

Ceske Budejovice is a small city of a hundred thousand on Czechoslovakia's Vltava River. Founded in 1265, it is now a provincial center for trade and light industry. The old-fashioned electric trolleys, supported by a maze of overhead wires and cables, evoked a childhood memory of visiting my grandmother in San Francisco, where I used to lie in bed at night all comfy and warm, listening to the sound of the trolleys coming up the hill.

As we waited in the lobby for our room assignments, it was apparent that this was the "in" place in town. Young people came and went from the big lobby bar, effortfully dressed to emulate western fashion. But they didn't know how to do it, as well as lacking the resources. The results were some of the strangest getups imaginable: all colors of jeans and high-top sneakers, young men in loose-fitting suits with T-shirts, flat-top haircuts, tattoos, and one earring. The young women were dressed in the sexiest outfits: high heels, short tight skirts, low-cut blouses, too much makeup, and puffed-up hair. They were serious, full of energy, and beautiful.

Not moving any too fast and wincing as the hot water hit the raw spots, I took longer than usual getting dressed. Nino grew impatient, so I told him to go on ahead. The moment the door closed behind him my mood lightened, throwing off the weight of the growing disapproval he pretended didn't exist.

At last there was no trace of the grueling day I'd just survived. I took extra pains with my make-up and arranged my hair as best I could. Not wanting to wear my only dress until the last day, I put on a red-and-pink striped T-shirt and a short black skirt, adding a little glamour with my gold hoop earrings and black sandals. Finally satisfied, I felt a whole lot better than I had an hour before.

At the entrance to the dining room, I hesitated a moment before entering. I felt gratified by the looks of admiration in the eyes of the men. Of course, it helped to be the only woman cycling, and I didn't know if they were admiring me or the fact of my survival. But hey, right now they made me feel beautiful.

The large dining room shone with the faded elegance of the 1920s. Burnished wood paneling gleamed in the dim light of the old chandeliers. A band was playing, and the sweet, plaintive sound of a Gypsy violin echoed as if from another time off the high, arched ceiling of the large dining room. Red-coated waiters stood at the sidelines, lounging and smoking.

I made my way across the room to the table where Nino was waiting, a dour expression on his face. He acknowledged my presence with a nod but didn't rise to seat me. I recognized with a pang of sadness that I'd traded one dream for another. As a couple, we'd taken the wrong fork in the road. I didn't want to think about it now, and wished we could have sat at one of the larger tables with the other cyclists.

The dinner was good, if plain, but at least there was enough of it.

Luigi was sitting at the head of a table directly in back of me. I half looked around, feeling his presence like a magnet.

Nino, following his own instincts, raised an eyebrow and launched into a discussion of how many of these men weren't very intelligent, especially Luigi. A moment later, the waiter arrived with two glasses of a special wine on a tray, indicating they were from Luigi.

I turned to see him admiring my transformation. I smiled my thanks and toasted him, enjoying his feelings through the taste of the wine.

Turning my attention back to Nino, I let myself be carried away by the hauntingly beautiful music, the abundant good food, and the aura of the past.

Dottore had hired a guide to take us on a walking tour of the town. My desire to learn about the town overcame my aches and pains; I tossed down more than my usual Advil, and we set off after dinner.

Our guide, Tatia, spoke Italian as well as some English. As we walked to the town square, people were getting on and off creaking trolleys; they looked tired. What work did they do? What kind of houses or apartments did they go home to? Ceske Budejovice was a pretty place, with small parks and spreading old shade trees. Our guide led us to the main square, which was the town's pride and joy. She said it was one of the most beautiful in Czechoslovakia, and so it was. Stylish old townhouses built close together surrounded the main square.

Tatia talked about some of the difficulties, now that they were free and had a mandate from the new Czechoslovakian government to privatize property and implement a market economy. One of the biggest problems, she said, was what to do about the houses of the town. The city was supposed to sell them. But they didn't know whether they should try to find the people who had owned them before the communists took over, or sell them to the people who were living in them, or sell them to other people with money who wanted to buy them. They hadn't the faintest idea how much money to ask for the houses, to whom the money should rightfully be paid, or how to go about actually doing it.

I blinked. It was hard to imagine people so isolated from, and innocent of, a market economy.

What would happen, she said, to the people living in the house if another person bought it? She couldn't imagine the government or anyone else actually putting someone out of their house. It just wouldn't be done, she said. I was glad I didn't have to solve this city's problems.

Gypsy music, good food, good cheer

An Affair of the Heart

Later, Nino and I went up to the hotel bar. It was dark, and the air was blue with smoke. We chose a table in a corner from which to survey the scene. Four prostitutes sat near the bar at what was probably their regular table. They were young, pretty, and hard. Their hair was bleached blonde, their lipstick too-bright red, their skirts tight and short, their white legs bare. Survival here didn't have the polite camouflage of more affluent countries. They smoked languidly, coldly assessing each prospect that walked in the door.

Their expressions changed when Luigi walked in. Covetously, their eyes followed him across the room, but Luigi appeared to be looking for his friends. "Nino," I said quickly, "please ask him to join us. I want to ask him some questions about cycling."

Nino hesitated for a brief second; I wondered if it was because he didn't like Luigi, or because he sensed a threat. But he waved, and Luigi sauntered over to join us. I thanked him for the wine. He asked if we had enjoyed it. I enjoyed it more than he knew. "Nino," I said, "please, just this once, translate exactly for me." Tired of translating, Nino often condensed a five-minute reply in Italian to a single sentence in English when he translated. But now it was important for me to know what Luigi really thought.

I asked him about techniques and timing for changing gears. He talked to me for a long time, with Nino translating. I listened with (I hoped) not too rapt attention, hoping Nino was not aware of the electricity passing between us. Lord, life was messy, sometimes.

Luigi asked Nino a question. Nino chuckled and told me Luigi wanted to know how I was able to go downhill so fast. Now it was my turn to be amused; I told Nino to tell him about my former ski-racing days when I'd been on the University of California Berkeley ski team and had raced in the veteran's class later at Squaw Valley. At this news Luigi appraised me anew, an eyebrow raised in surprise.

He said, "You do extremely well on the flat, but you fall apart on the hills. You must push yourself more on the hills and cycle through the burn." He said his group had tried to shake me off a couple of times on the flat, but had been unable to do so. I thought back to those occasions and laughed, remembering hanging on to the back of Luigi's lead group as if my life depended on it. I'd wondered if they were trying to drop me or if they were just that fast all the time.

I asked Nino to ask him if he minded my asking about his cycling life. Mixed feelings flashed across Luigi's face, or perhaps it was my intuition; I sensed that he didn't care much for Nino but wanted to talk to me.

He began to open up; I knew this was unusual for him. He'd started racing in his teens. His family had been too poor to own a bicycle, but whenever he could get his hands on one he was always first uphill. Whenever he rode uphill, he said, power kicked into his legs and he took off like a shot. He worked and saved, and bought his first racing bike one part at a time. Training all the time, he became an outstanding climber. After wining local races, he started to train for the big races. Knowing he could run away from everybody in the hills, he figured he didn't need any help. He trained alone, and raced alone. Unable to attract a sponsor because he was such a loner, he had to train after work. But he said he enjoyed being a dark horse, and he entered the professional cycling world not by invitation but by forced acceptance after winning several important races.

My first impressions of him had been on the mark: he really was like a wild animal—not to be tamed or molded by man, woman, culture, or organization—and he'd gladly take the consequences in exchange for his individual freedom.

As he finished speaking, I wondered how to phrase the question I wanted most to ask. Too often I'd been defeated by the sight alone of a mountain we had to climb, and I wanted to know how he thought about it. "Luigi," I said, "In your mind, how do you think about the hills?"

He sipped his drink, and looked at me for a long time. Finally he answered, "I don't see them. Cycling, after all, is an affair of the heart." His answer pierced me like an arrow, flooding me anew with the passion I felt for the sport. *Yes.*

Cycling had reached deep into my heart now. So had he.

12

Day Six: Ceske Budejovice to Prague, 97 miles

Bad Morning

After breakfast, Nino shrugged off my suggestion that we clean our grit-clogged chains. So gathering up what paper napkins I could find, I left breakfast early and went out to the garages, where a small group of the more experienced cyclists was cleaning the mud off their own bikes. I found the chain lubricant I'd brought and set to work.

They all stopped to see if I knew how to do this, which I did (cleaning things being so foreign to women and all). Finished, I raised my greasy hands and said, "*Eh,*" an extremely useful Italian exclamation that means: *Oh my God, It is what it is, It isn't my fault, It's God's will, Get a load of this, What the hell do I do now?* or whatever the moment calls for, and someone handed me a hotel towel.

We'd start early today, to allow time to visit a village where there was a family connection. While we were standing in the pack waiting to take off, I caught Old Luigi's eye. He greeted me as he did every morning, "*Tutto* okay?" I laughed and gave him the thumb's up. Having made it this far, we were both in great high spirits. If there ever was a picture of Italian grit and spirit, it was Old Luigi. He was tanned brown as a saddle and wore no socks with his cycling shoes, which were falling apart with age and use. His spindly legs were a little bowed, and his carefully trimmed mustache gave him a sort of Chaplinesque air. He reminded me of an old olive tree: thick, gnarled, and tough. Though he'd discarded the head bandage from his fall, the long gash on his forehead was still fresh, and large black and yellow bruises framed his laughing blue eyes. His cycling cap was dirty and crushed almost beyond recognition. He wore it like a badge of honor.

We'd no sooner started off when Nino announced he'd forgotten to return his room key, so I agreed to wait for him. Somehow he forgot, didn't hear, or chose to ignore that I'd wait. Standing beside the road in the quiet drizzle, I noticed how threadbare the city looked in the gray of the morning—in need of paint, street repair, and a million other things.

As I began to worry I'd never catch up with the group, a couple of cyclists who'd gotten a late start came along and I drafted them through the wet streets of the still-sleeping city, over slick trolley tracks, spitting out dirty water thrown up from potholes, back to the group.

The fast pull to the group turned me into a lactic acid factory. Gritting my teeth, I pressed on, trying to spin my pedals fast to work the pain caused by the lactic acid out of my legs. It took everything I could muster to hang onto the rear of the group. Then I felt the hand on my back. Luigi! How could he come up behind me when he always started off at the head of the pack? A backward glance found concern on his face.

"*Giorno duro per me*" ("Hard day for me"), I said.

"*No! Giorno facile!*" ("No, an easy day!"), he said, trying to cheer me up. "*Non ci sono salite oggi*" ("There will be no hills today"), he said. "*Canta!*" ("Sing!"), he commanded. He must have heard I'd been singing on my bicycle, to make the time pass. Singing made me happy; every memory of it brought me joy. When I was little, I'd sing along with the popular singers on the radio or stereo, and I'd sing in the woods as I tramped along, smelling the trees. I'd belt out

"Old Man River" in the shower. I'd drive my family crazy practicing "The Yodeling Boogie" to sing in school talent shows, before I learned about Sarah Vaughn and jazz. I remembered one night in the late sixties. Divorced with two children, I drove to one of my first gigs as a professional singer, smiling, thinking how it felt like cheating to get paid for doing what I loved so much.

So I sang, as Luigi pushed me. As always, it made me feel better. After the song was over he motioned he had to get back to the front, and accelerated ahead. Our encounters were more frequent now but always casual, with few words exchanged.

I learned more about Luigi by listening to pieces of conversation at dinners. An outsider in the world of bicycle racing, his friends were fiercely loyal to him, but he was intensely disliked by team-oriented people. In Italy, not being a team player is akin to spitting in the eye of society. He was a great climber; everyone knew he was champion material. He trained hard, played hard, drank hard, chased women, and thumbed his nose at everybody.

Becoming a top-ranked *corridore* at the zenith of his racing career, suddenly and with no explanation, he quit. *No one* quits racing when they are winning. Why? Rumors flew. They said no one would sponsor him; he'd developed a heart murmur; he couldn't afford to race without a sponsor; he lost his will; no team would have him; he lost his nerve; he was just crazy.

I wondered if I'd ever know. Whatever it was, Luigi didn't seem to me like a man who was carrying around a burden, and least of all would he care what people said about him.

Luigi pushed me up to Nino, who to my surprise was cycling in the middle of the group. He must have passed me in town without my seeing him.

"Nino," I suggested, "I know you usually like to cycle in the rear, and I like to cycle up front so I'll have groups to fall back to, but shouldn't we have sort of an informal buddy system?" He shrugged, ignoring that he hadn't bothered to look for me after having asked me to wait. I continued, "Even though we don't usually cycle together, I always have a rough idea of where in the group you probably are. I guess I'd feel better if I knew you loosely kept track of where in the group I probably am."

"Sure, okay," he said.

I didn't know whether that was a real or feigned agreement. *Just don't get lost*, I told myself.

The Village

We spread out on the almost empty roads, across the flat plains of Czechoslovakia. The countryside seemed dreary and lonely—perhaps it was just the perpetually gray sky. It rained now and then. We passed no towns or settlements—just mile after undulating mile of empty plains and forest.

A buzz went around in the group indicating our village stop was just ahead. Years ago, a young man fled from this village and the drab, go-nowhere life of communist society, and settled in northern Italy, in San Pietro in Cariano. He was not with us, but he'd arranged for us to stop at the home of his mother, who was expecting us. It was a relief to see the village and dispel the feeling of cycling continually through the middle of nowhere.

We turned down a side road bounded by plain, neatly kept small houses with well-tended gardens, and were met at the small church by a group comprising surely every citizen in the village.

Dottore made a grand speech about our *ponte per l'Europa unita*, and adopted the village as a new sister city to San Pietro in Cariano. There were hugs and tears, and more speeches.

Trays bearing cups of wine were passed around. Some of the cups were antique demitasses of the most delicate china—people's treasures. I prayed none would get broken. Village women pinned little Czech flags on our shirts. There were many toasts, in Czech and

Italian. The principal of the local school, who spoke a little English and Italian, translated for the villagers.

Tugging on Nino's arm, I implored him to translate. He'd grown tired of this, and was too busy listening. So I watched. Most of the villagers were blond, their faces fair and full of hope. There was an earnestness in their honest and open faces that believed Dottore's words about the possibility of a united Europe, and that they, at last, could be part of it.

Most of the group continued on to the mother's house; but a few of us, at the invitation of the village doctor and the school principal, went to see the local school. The principal was a thoughtful man with intelligent eyes. He apologized for the poverty of the little school. The village and the school buildings may have been poor, but the school didn't look so poor in terms of teaching, or in their obvious commitment to the education of their children.

The children's neat writing and art was pinned up on one wall. Other walls were covered with maps and teaching materials, and the shelves were filled with books. Of course, I had no idea what was in the books. Perhaps part of the poverty to which they alluded was the lack of freedom to teach other than what the Soviet hierarchy had dictated. I didn't feel free to ask this central question on such short acquaintance.

The principal told us about the 1968 Prague Spring, the Soviet invasion that quashed the blossoming liberalization of the country, and the intervening years of fear and stagnation when dissident intellectuals, with Vaclav Havel as a leading voice, were smuggling their writings and ideas out of the country.

By 1988 the up-swelling of dissent had reached critical mass. Czech intellectuals and dissidents came together to form the political party of freedom, the Civic Forum, in 1988. Vaclav Havel was elected president in 1989. Freedom had been worth everything, the principal said. "When our minds are imprisoned, we might as well be dead."

He removed his glasses and gazed at me intently; "Tell me about the idea of America."

"The idea of America is freedom," I said. "America is an immense and diverse country. Though predominantly white with European roots, we are fast becoming a more multicultural and multiethnic society. Great numbers of people immigrate from all over the world. There is a sometimes clashing mix of cultural traditions, causing a constant rearranging of society and its norms, weaving a rich and complex fabric of the American culture to come. But everyone holds in common a belief in life's possibilities in a free society. Everyone came to America for freedom and a better life. This can-do spirit and fierce love of freedom are the glue that holds Americans together. We've died to protect this freedom," I said, "and we always will."

The principal stopped. Tears rolled down his cheeks from under his round-rimmed wire glasses, and he couldn't speak. Freedom is all the more precious to those who've been denied it. I took his arm, wishing we could have spent an evening with these educated and quietly refined people, and we walked on.

By now we were beginning to worry about reaching Prague even in time for dinner. As we pedaled off, I glanced back at our new friends waving from the little school, its drabness masquerading its higher values.

Merging onto the main road, we met the other cyclists coming from the village mother's house, where wine must have flowed freely. Some of them were singing and weaving, their bicycles tracing a slalom unsteadily on the road. They sang, laughed, and wobbled; I didn't envy the hangovers they'd have tomorrow.

Some of the men sang beautifully. There were several operatic-quality baritones in the group, and a few tenors. Occasionally one of them would burst forth with some wonderful Italian song. Stocky Giovanni, with calves almost as wide as he was tall, sang in a beautiful tenor. He also yodeled, amusing everyone by imitating the Austrians.

More often now, Luigi would ride up and motion me to draft him for awhile, slowing his pace a little so I could do it. I sang for him words he couldn't understand, but feelings he could. He'd turn his head and flash me a smile. Today he rode up, put his now-familiar hand on my back, and swept me forward. As a performer, "Golden Earrings" had always been my favorite and most deeply felt song. Into the wind, I sang it for him now. Then we rode on in silence, each of us experiencing the frustration of not being able to talk to each other. He nodded and moved on.

Often when I found myself cycling alone, I'd become aware that Bruno was behind me, just being there to see if I was okay. A backward glance confirmed he was there now. He liked my singing too, he said. He had the radiant smile of a man who feels a friend to God—the kind of man who would take responsibility to care for whoever needed it, in his quiet way. He pedaled with me for long stretches, gently chiding me when I shifted down too far, teaching me with his years of experience and the caring of his heart. Every morning, I saw him cross himself and pray for our day's safe passage.

The men were tired, a few still riding a little unsteadily. They reached out to each other on their bikes—a pat on the back, a shoulder squeezed in encouragement, a friendly poke.

Bruno moved on, and I pedaled alone for awhile. Several of the men were in the habit of giving me their best "come hither" looks as we pedaled. Franco and Alberto pulled up alongside, giving me the full treatment. Franco was the tall blond from Switzerland who hadn't trained for the trip but who seemed to be doing fine now, and Alberto was one of the handsomest men in the group. He looked in his forties, with graying black hair and the sexiest eyes I'd ever seen. Last night at dinner I'd asked if the calluses on his hands were from cycling.

"No," he said, "I'm a shoemaker, and the calluses are from putting shoes onto the anvil."

Now they flirted shamelessly; I laughed and gave it right back to them, enjoying myself to the hilt. The drab countryside needed all the game-playing we could muster up.

Long Countryside

Our plan had been to cycle the approximately eighty more-or-less flat miles to Prague by mid-afternoon, including the village stop. Then we would tour the city.

The more I cycled with the group, the more androgynous I became. Flirting aside, the fact that I was a woman faded while we were on the road into the other qualities we all shared. I took on the same road dirt, the same fatigue, the same love of the sport, the same excitement in the adventure as the men. Those whom I knew respected my effort and treated me like an equal, at least in the milieu of "cyclist," suspended for the moment from that of "the rest of the world."

The countryside stretched out so endlessly that it took on the feeling of cycling over a continent. Rolling grasslands and occasional forests spread out before us, blending gray skies, intermittent rain, and the wet, empty road into one dreamy, hypnotic landscape. Sometimes I'd lose myself in it, and forget for a moment which country I was in. Occasionally a truck would go by, spewing noxious fumes. I amused myself with important issues, such as which blouse I'd wear with which skirt for our tour of Prague.

Lost in thought in the quiet of the day and the mesmerizing white line painted down the center of the road, I instinctively hit the brakes as a crash occurred ahead. Beppe had gone down for no apparent reason, twenty meters in front of me. Instantly I was there, with others, and we were off our bikes to see if we could help. Beppe, a giant of a man with an affable nature, sat up, somewhat dazed, and was checking himself over to see if he had any injuries. The line beside the road had been freshly painted. Beppe had accidentally drifted into it and his bike had slipped out from under him. He was covered with fresh white paint, now mingling with blood from the road rash on his legs, arms, and face. What a mess! His beautiful bike was also full of white paint and scratches. There'd been no warning markers—nothing. It could have happened to any of us.

Beppe managed a smile, realizing his injuries were superficial. Dottore waited with him until the van arrived with the medical supplies. I wondered how long it would take for all that paint to wear off. At home, he'd have the only white scabs in Italy. I wished I could say that in Italian. Probably just as well I couldn't.

Since more than a few hangovers were in full swing, it was decided to make an unscheduled rest stop, and we made ourselves at home in an open field. My calves were cramping badly and I plopped down on a log, grasping my legs.

Luigi, who always watched me now out of the corner of his eye, came over and without asking, knelt down and went to work massaging my calves, to sidelong looks from a few of the men. He kneaded the muscles deeply, and when I winced he glanced up and dug in harder. My curiosity about him was almost unbearable.

Why had he quit racing? This wasn't the time to ask. But I would find out. Somehow.

Finally the knots relaxed, and all I could feel was the rhythmic massage of his strong hands, sending a thrill all the way up my spine. God, I never wanted a man so much. Others were watching, and he didn't look up.

He called Bruno over and asked him to tell me that I must learn to massage my own legs to knead out the cramps, as he'd shown me. I thanked him, and our eyes met. I was his for that moment, and he knew it.

Morning crept into afternoon. Eighty miles came and went. Having programmed myself for that far only, I felt cheated when

Prague didn't materialize. Peering into the distance, I expected it to suddenly appear, like a mirage, in the distance. Eventually it did, but not until ninety-seven miles.

Then, to my great dismay, word filtered back that we'd tour Prague by bicycle, before going to the hotel. Bitterly disappointed, I'd looked forward to seeing Prague in my female persona. But keeping up was all I could think about. I never did get in sync cycling with the group today, and now just staying with them required all of my concentration.

Adventures in Prague

Prague is a fabulous place, one of the few great cities in Europe that has never been destroyed by war. It is so beautiful and cosmopolitan, with its grand piazzas and elegant, multistoried townhouses, that I was stunned by the contrast with the scant, poor villages of the drab countryside through which we'd pedaled. Not only was it like entering a completely intact medieval city, but one that had been sleeping for forty years.

Now in 1990, only a year after the Velvet Revolution liberated Czechoslovakia from Soviet communism, Prague was still relatively quiet; it had been discovered by adventurous travelers but not yet by tourists. It was possible to imagine ourselves back in the fourteenth century when the city had been one of the leading cultural and trade centers of Central Europe, entering the city on horseback instead of on bicycles.

The centuries-old, ornate buildings were kept as if new, freshly painted with new shutters and fixtures. The piazzas were immense and lined with cafés, and the lofty cathedrals rivaled any in Europe.

Only the cobblestone streets looked as ancient as they were, with stones the size of bricks, rounded with age and use. Many were broken with sharp edges, and it was not unusual to find spaces of two inches between them. Our skinny-tired racing bikes, their high-pressure tires transferring every bump up your spine to rattle your brain in your skull, were the worst possible vehicles from which to see Prague. I was torn between not looking at the huge cobblestones because the sight of them scared me, and having to watch where I was going every second.

Suddenly we found ourselves in a trolley tunnel, pedaling in a dark, two-foot corridor between the trolley tracks and the curb. Once out of the tunnel, we had to negotiate a tangled maze of trolley tracks. In the middle of a busy intersection, trying to cross the maze of slick tracks as perpendicularly as possible, my wheel slipped into a space between the track and the cobblestones, slowing me and throwing me off balance. To keep from falling, I yanked my foot out of the toe clip and put it down, thinking I'd caught myself, but my cleat slipped on the track and I fell anyway. Pedestrians were crossing everywhere, distracted by my fall as I struggled up, slipping and sliding. Policemen were frantically blowing whistles for everybody to stop, which no one did. Finally upright, I straggled to the rear of the group, assuring everyone that I was fine. "God, this is really fun," I bitched into the wind, knowing no one could understand me. *Just survive this*, I thought, *and someday I'll get back to Prague and see it in a less death-defying manner.*

At last we crossed the famous Charles Bridge spanning the Vltava River that bisects the city. The bridge had been built in the fifteenth century, and motor traffic was no longer allowed on it. Both sides of the bridge were lined with musicians and people selling curios. Not able to let my gaze drift as we crossed, my ears caught a string quartet, a flautist, and the plaintive melody of a Gypsy guitar. Out of the corner of my eye, they looked about a song away from an empty stomach. Other young eastern Europeans (you could always tell by their clothes) lounged about, looking poor, thin, tough, and full of hope.

A lone bicycle tourist from somewhere in the East stopped to watch us. He was young and strong with thick, tousled black hair, high color, and clear, searching dark eyes, betraying a hint of the East. I wondered if he was from one of the Soviet provinces. His heavy bicycle was like nothing I'd ever seen, surely weighing more than fifty pounds, with heavily spoked wheels. He carried a big canvas rucksack on his back and a heavy, cumbersome canvas tent on the back of his bicycle, with long tent stakes tied on the side. People will go to incredible lengths to see the world; such is the human wanderlust.

Two ornately carved spires decorated the end of the cobblestone bridge, through which we passed to enter the oldest part of the city leading up to the Castle. We wound uphill through narrow stone streets lined with tiny shops selling antiques and art on our way to Prague Castle, the presidential residence.

I continued to straggle a little behind and probably would not have made it up the hill to the castle except for Bruno and a few others already on top cheering me on, "*Vai, vai, Lina, la ultima salita!*"

The stone-paved square facing the castle complex was enormous, surrounded by Prague Castle and government buildings. An elaborate, tall, wrought-iron fence trimmed in gold surrounded the castle. I knew castles only from the *Grimm's Fairy Tales* of my childhood, and seeing the rectangular, large castle building was somewhat of a letdown. I guess I'd expected spires, flags, drawbridges, and a moat.

Pictures and backslapping over, it was time for the big moment; we were ready to present the bicycle to President Vaclav Havel. The bicycle had traveled safely in one of the vans, and most of us hadn't seen it yet.

Dottore, gathering us all around, went into one of the vans and reverently wheeled out President Vaclav Havel's bicycle. A wonder it was: De Rosa's finest, with the best Campagnolo components. It was Italian through and through, one of the finest bicycles possible. I squinted against the brilliance of it in the afternoon sun; or maybe I was just blinded by my vision of President Vaclav Havel pedaling it around Prague. It was painted the palest, most delicate, metallic sky blue. The seat was of the softest deerskin-colored suede, and the handlebars were suede-wrapped in a darker shade of blue.

It was decided to set out our lunch right here in front of the castle gate while Dottore rang to talk to an aide, to see if President Havel was here to receive the bicycle. The president wasn't at home, and wasn't expected until the next morning. We were disappointed, but it was decided that we'd try again in the morning to present the bicycle.

Meanwhile, just as we were attacking lunch with our customary gusto, the castle police arrived to tell us we couldn't eat lunch there or anywhere else in the castle complex square, and that we'd have to leave.

But, Dottore and Antonio explained with gestures, we were already eating. Couldn't they see that? Of course they only spoke Czech, and we only spoke Italian. But the communication was clear.

Out.

But how could we? After all, we were, sacrosanct to an Italian, *eating*. More castle police were called. We resolutely refused to understand their unreasonable request due to not understanding their language.

The castle police apparently had never encountered a situation quite like this before, where sixty Italians refused to stop eating their lunch in front of the gates to Prague Castle. Seeing that we wouldn't take their orders seriously, they became confused, and didn't know what to do. We munched our *panini*, enjoying the show, while they huddled in conference.

Finally one came over to Dottore with a drawing of a clock, showing a half hour from now, and a picture of bicycles and stick figures behind the bars of a jail. He held it up to Dottore's face, and patted the gun at his side.

Dottore, knowing when discretion was the better part of valor, readily agreed. Oreste was about to offer the head cop a glass of wine, but someone, thank God, clapped a hand over his mouth. We tried not to laugh, but there was a lot of giggling behind hands. In exactly half an hour and not a minute less, we were on our way to the hotel.

Before we left the castle square, some of us, led by Dottore, visited St. Vitus Cathedral inside the castle complex. The light shining through the stained glass windows shimmered with brilliance. The magnificent mosaic of the windows reflected and magnified every color of the spectrum. The whole inside of the cathedral was criss-crossed with rays of light. It was like being inside a giant prism, and it had the effect of bathing everyone who entered with light and joy in the sheer beauty of the place. My heart sang, just being there.

Our hotel was on a hill outside the center of town. It was large, modern, expensive, and boring. But I was happy to be there; I was glad to be anywhere in the evenings as long as it wasn't on the seat of a bicycle.

I loved dinnertime because I felt like a woman again and because I'd survived another day. Transformed again for the evening, I took Nino's arm as we strolled across the hotel's expansive and richly furnished lobby bar, looking for a spot to settle in for some serious people-watching. I was accustomed to people's puzzled glances as they tried to figure out my nationality, not apparent in my looks. I'd always turned heads; I was not quite beautiful, but my strong spirit imbued my bearing. Fit and vibrant in early middle age, I was tall, with dark hair, steady blue eyes, an angular face, and a long nose. I was often mistaken for a German in Italy, and an Italian in Germany.

Settling into a couple of comfortable leather chairs and at ease with each other, Nino and I agreed to make peace for the rest of the trip in the unspoken knowledge that we were stuck with each other and might as well make the best of it. I sincerely prayed I could get to Warsaw without doing him bodily harm. And he, I think, hoped the same. More and more, he was at a loss to know what to do about me; whenever his frustration level reached a certain pitch he'd say, "What am I to do with you, Lina?" (As if I were his to do anything with.) I pictured him trying to figure out into which drawer of his consciousness to put me: woman according to Nino, or woman according to apparent reality—or into which drawer of his emotional life: lover, friend, or pain in the ass.

Of course we never discussed any of this. We were too damn tired. Instead, we settled down and drank a toast to the adventure, while we watched the comings and goings of international business-men accompanied by elegant ladies who I highly doubted were their wives. I hoped I could return here someday, in a more old-world atmosphere, with time on my hands.

Mario and Memories

Mario ambled by, and Nino invited him to join us. The conversa-tion turned to training, with Mario recalling his earlier training days when he was racing. I asked him to tell us more about his past cycling life, and Nino translated as he talked.

Like many of the others, Mario had enjoyed an early career in bicycle racing, sparked by tales of Coppi and Bartoli on the family radio. By the age of eight, the desire to be a *corridore* had taken him over. When he started to race at fifteen, he won regularly, soon winning the championship for the region of Verona. He became a *dilettante* (ranking amateur), the class just before *professionista*. He followed his passion until a noncycling accident brought his racing career to an end when he was twenty. But he said he was very happy that he'd had the opportunity to race, and that he did well.

As Nino translated, I reflected that feeling sorry for oneself is not something a cyclist does. A cyclist takes the risks, reaping whatever glory, pain, or other price is asked along the way.

Now Mario is retired and does what he loves best: he designs and makes bicycle frames in a small shop near his home, and he trains junior racers. *Il ciclismo agonistico* (bicycle racing), he told us, has the greatest spread of suffering and joy, the greatest test of the *volonta* (will) of any sport. His own passion for cycling is as strong as ever, he said, but now he rides only for the love of it, and to help junior racers develop their potential.

His enthusiasm grew as he told us how you have to start training with eight-year-olds, because eight to sixteen are the ages during which the aspiring young racers become socialized. They organize them into teams that can win, so they can experience success and begin to think they can be champions. He said that without this help they can't become champions; they can't do it alone. After age eighteen, cycling is a team discipline. When an untrained thirteen-year-old with raw talent wins a race, he thinks only of himself. When he's nineteen or twenty, he's easily defeated if he hasn't been socialized to think as a team, because he isn't prepared to suffer, to rise from defeat. Confidence and a strong will build gradually for the thirteen-year-old who has grown up with a team; even when he loses, he knows his turn will come if he works hard enough.

Caught off guard, I sat transfixed. Tears suddenly burned my eyes. My father died when I was fourteen. I still liked to say that at least I had him until I was almost fifteen.

I loved sports from the beginning, but there was one little problem. I wasn't very well-coordinated. My father had to teach me how to run, how to coordinate my arms and legs. It hadn't escaped me that the other kids did this quite naturally. When I pointed this out he'd tell me, "That's okay, sometimes you have to work a little harder than other people to learn something, but you can always do it. Practice more," he'd say. "Figure out how you were doing it wrong, practice doing it right, and try again. You absolutely will learn; remember that in your heart." So I practiced running by myself, not wanting to show off my lack of natural skill to the other kids. I knew I couldn't play baseball until I could run. So I ran and ran, and learned that I could learn.

As he taught me how to play baseball, he taught me the discipline to practice, to train for a sport. Every night after work he'd play catch with me for an hour, never laughing when I tripped over my feet trying to make a catch. Later he helped me train to be a distance swimmer, the sport I was doing when he died. The seed had been planted. I knew what I had to do to become a competitive athlete. But he was gone. I trained alone, with the gift of his legacy.

More painful memories surfaced of my own two sons, who grew up without this kind of support from a father. Since my own chosen sports had been individual efforts, I wasn't the one to teach them how to be part of a team or to suffer, because I didn't know how myself. And there was no one else to teach them. The pain in my heart flashed back to the day my oldest son came home in tears and frustrated rage because he couldn't make his new kite fly, and the other kids in the park had their fathers to show them. And to the first day of Little League practice when I physically dragged my younger son down to the baseball field because he'd changed his mind about going, and I told him he had to go at least once in exchange for having bought him the damn forty-dollar mitt. We needed a father. We didn't have one. I taught them as best I could, steered them into team sports in school, but the void was never filled.

The news wasn't all bad, though. With guidance from me, school coaches, and their own natural inclinations, both boys became superb athletes. The younger made the all-stars in Little League, and became a great golfer by caddying and cajoling men at the local course to teach him. The older, now a black belt in martial arts, found masters to teach him on his own. He did a century ride at thirteen and only told me later. Both of them are expert mountain bikers and skiers. One year, the three of us won the family slalom race at a ski resort, triumphing over even the families with fathers.

Sipping our drinks while we watched the passing parade, I smiled, remembering that race; it was one of my very proudest moments.

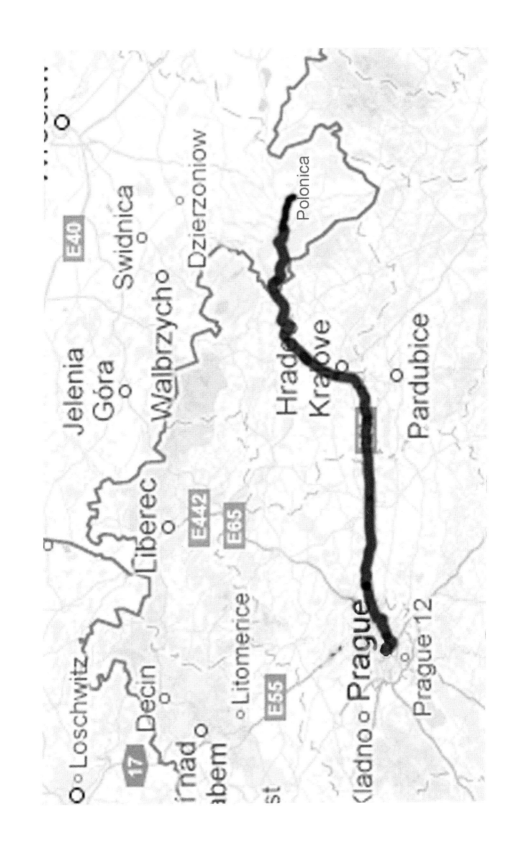

13

DAY SEVEN: PRAGUE TO POLONICA, 116 MILES

Lost Already?

At breakfast, Dottore told us we might as well prepare for a late start this morning, because he couldn't call the presidential residence at Prague Castle until nine o'clock to see if President Havel had returned so we could present him the bicycle. *Ahhh*, I sighed contentedly, looking around the ludicrously elegant (for us) dining room, and poured myself a second cup of coffee.

In the parking garage with our bikes and ready to go, we continued to wait. At last Dottore returned and told us sadly that President Havel had not yet returned. The aide had offered to give the bike to President Havel for us; but for an Italian, a presentation without ceremony, the exchange of goodwill, and at least one little speech would be unthinkable. So it was decided that the group would stop here on the way back in the vans and buses, to try again to present the bicycle.

It was almost ten before we were finally on the road, and a hundred-mile-plus day lay ahead. At least, word had it, the terrain would be flat until we crossed the border into Poland, where we'd begin our climb into the Carpathian Mountains.

The problem with negotiating eastern European cities, according to our navigator/drivers, was that although we had road maps, we'd arrive too late in the day and leave too early the next day to acquire a city map. So this time, to avoid any possible risk of getting lost, Dottore simply hired a taxi to lead us out of town. What an Italian solution!

If this had been an American group, we wouldn't have moved until six men had consulted their maps and figured how to do it without ever asking for help or directions. I got the giggles and couldn't stop laughing at the sight of all fifty-four of us parading proudly through Prague, the yellow taxi in the lead.

The men looked at me strangely, not finding this unusual or especially funny. Over the past days, I'd noticed that things I thought were funny didn't amuse the Italians, and things I didn't consider funny at all drove them into fits of frenzied laughter. They thought it was especially funny when I'd try to say something serious in Italian. They'd try to listen with a straight face, but they couldn't do it. I never realized humor was so cultural. Their favorite joke was to poke fun at each other, which they did without mercy, laughing uproariously.

Soon after the taxi left us, the dark sky opened up and dumped itself upon us. It was a deluge. One of the group I was riding with spotted a covered bus stop. We made a beeline for it, stuffing thirteen Italian men, one mangy, damp American woman, and most of our bicycles into it. We watched it pour. They were telling dirty jokes—I didn't have to understand the words to figure that out—and glancing over at me to be sure I didn't understand. They snickered and guffawed, and I watched the steam rise from their shoulders. I pretended not to have any idea what they were talking about, as I fished some bread and cheese out of my pocket and munched contentedly in a corner.

Finally the rain let up enough for us to start again, but drafting became a problem due to road water being thrown up by rear wheels. It would splatter me in a stripe up the front of my jacket, and in the face. I used my finger as a windshield wiper for my glasses. Spitting the road grit out of my teeth, I chose two men cycling together and rode behind and between them. *Hah!* This worked fine. They looked like they'd been stomping in mud puddles, and if I looked as grungy as they did no one would be able to tell if I were even a female anymore, just like Nino had said.

We congratulated ourselves on negotiating the outskirts of Prague without getting lost. Following the vans, we had just turned east onto the road proclaiming itself toward the Polish border when, unbelievably, the road simply ended in a field. The vans screeched to a halt and we dismounted and walked around in circles. Someone said, "*Ci siamo gia perduti?*" ("Are we lost already?") This was less funny than it might have been, because it was true. Maps were brought out, bananas were munched, heads were scratched. Fortuitously, a tall, thin farmer in a straw hat and coveralls pedaled up to us on a creaky old bicycle and offered to help. After a lengthy map conference with the farmer, we were again on our way.

The plains of northern Czechoslovakia lay before us. My God, the world was a big place! The sun poked in and out of clouds heavy with rain. Funny how important clouds become in your world when you're out on a bicycle; they portend your immediate future, telling of winds, storms, or a gentle day, filling you with wonder, dread, anxiety, or joy.

We fell easily into the regular rhythm of our day. The men chatted, told jokes, or just pedaled. Every once in a while we'd pass through a village. Most were poor and plain, but one village had a picturesque town square lined with trees and once-fine houses behind neglected gardens. Leaning against a bronze monument in the square, teenagers waved and cheered as we passed.

Noticing how the village streets were paved in cobblestones, I thought this not only charming but practical. Later, learning that cobblestone streets still existed only because there was no money to pave over them, I felt chagrined at not having been able to distinguish charm from poverty.

As we whooshed through another village, an old woman in a faded green babushka stood on her small porch with her hands over her ears, her face distorted with fear. I wondered if she was reliving the Soviet invasion of August 1968. Maybe the quiet approach of our bicycles on the innocent spring day reminded her of the stealth of the advance Soviet guard that preceded the tanks. Maybe they came over this very road. I tried to feel her fear, but as an American whose home country has never been invaded, I could not.

Every once in a while someone would invite me to draft, and I'd get on their wheel for awhile. Luigi dropped back to check on me, and his smile always gave me a surge of energy. Bruno gave me a push, and then Luigino pushed. I felt strong and didn't need any help today, but I loved their offers of help and would never turn them down.

The fact that I was getting stronger and had less trouble keeping up had mixed reviews from the men. I wanted to be liked by everyone, and I hoped they'd be glad I was getting stronger. At the same time I knew that was naive, given my experience with male egos.

There were a few men who so disliked my presence on the trip that they radiated hostility. A few nights ago I'd stood next to Gianni while we waited for a hotel elevator. He was a big man, a strong rider, and as macho as they come. He steadfastly had always refused to look at or speak to me. I'd smiled at him in vain as he looked right through me. "Leave it alone," Nino had advised. But it wasn't my nature.

Gianni and I had been alone in the elevator. He looked as if he'd rather be anywhere but there. I said, "*Sono ciclista. Non e culpa mia se sono donna.*" ("I am a cyclist. It is not my fault that I am a woman.") Again he ignored me, but I knew this would baffle him and he'd think about it, hating that I made him think about it. I loved tweaking arrogant machismo.

Luigino and Arturo

Luigino was one of the stronger riders, and usually rode up front with Luigi. He was an old friend of Luigi's from their racing days. Today he rode up and tried to tell me something. He took care to speak slowly so I could understand. But he spoke in the same heavy Veneto dialect as Luigi and I couldn't understand him, so it took him a couple of tries with gestures to make me understand that I should avoid cycling on the painted lines in the road when the pavement was wet, because they became dangerously slippery. At home, I'd adopted the habit of riding the white line on roads without shoulders to keep out of traffic, and I must have been doing it unconsciously here. A kind man, Luigino had gone out of his way to tell me this. He was tall and dark, a big man. Whenever I'd caught a glimpse of him, he was always smiling. He worked hard; it was written on his hands and in the lines of his handsome, rough face. And he loved life; you could hear it in his laugh, sense it in his contagious good nature. Since he seemed willing to take the trouble to speak slowly to me, I motioned Bruno, who was nearby, to pedal with us and help translate. I asked about his life in bicycle racing.

He'd been driving trucks for thirty years, Luigino said, but cycling had always been his passion. Like the others, he was raised listening to the exploits of Coppi and Bartoli on the family radio, and he dreamed of becoming a great racer, a *corridore*, like them.

He worked and saved to buy his first racing bike, a Bottechia with the first Campagnolo *cambio* (gear changer). In those days, he said, races were much harder than they are now because most of the roads were unpaved, and it wasn't uncommon to race in mud, rocks, gravel, and over cobblestones. There were always huge holes in the roads. Bicycles were much heavier then, and the tires bigger. You had to be strong and tough, he told me, because you were always falling in holes or in the mud. Frequently mud would clog the *cambio*. If this happened, the wheel would just stop. If you hadn't already been thrown over the handlebars, you'd get off, pick up the bike, and shake it hard to get the stones and dirt out. If that didn't work, you'd pick it up and bounce it on the ground to clear the *cambio*, remount, and continue on your way in the race.

He began racing at eighteen. He'd come home after work, eat, and go out and train until or after dark every night, advancing rapidly to become a *professionista*. From 1949 to 1951 he competed in the big races with Luigi and Arturo. There were no team cars then, and they changed their own tires during races. He used to time himself changing tires at home on rainy nights, setting a personal record of one-and-a-half minutes. He loved the thrill and the danger of riding close in a pack, the adrenalin rush of competition. Cycling still excites him as much as it did in his racing days; but now, he said, his greatest thrill is exploring new places and riding the roads in eastern Europe on which he'd driven a truck for so many years.

We'd been pedaling on the vast, open plain for hours. Luigino saw I was tiring. We always seemed to travel at a speed that was just a little more than I could sustain. He suggested I draft him, which I gratefully did. I slipped into place close behind his wheel, secure in the knowledge that he would ride smoothly, ever aware of my presence. I wondered where Nino was; I hadn't seen him since the start. We rode into the wind, but Luigino always maintained the same speed, cutting it like a bulldozer. I enjoyed the silent camaraderie, all of us loving the wind and the journey, silently, each in his own way.

The headwind turned into a crosswind, fingers of gusts snatching capriciously at our wheels. Luigino motioned me to the side. I pulled myself up to forty-five degrees of him, until I found the calm spot in the slipstream. I rode in the protected spot for a long time, moving forward and back as the wind changed, to keep in the slipstream; I could feel it when I found the right spot. The pedaling was hard, but I felt protected; this helped me and made me stronger.

We rode behind Arturo and his friends, who were in the lead

group. Arturo, still known affectionately as *il biondo* (the blond), was the most famous *corridore* in the group, nationally known. He'd raced in the Giro d'Italia. He was a compact, muscular man who appeared much younger than his sixty-some years, because of his great energy and garrulous good nature. His now sand-gray hair was close-cropped, framing blue eyes and a strong, friendly face.

Nino and I had gone to see Arturo before the trip to inspect the bicycle he'd ridden in the Giro, which Arturo had offered to loan Nino until he could acquire a bicycle here. Nino, star struck at the prospect of riding a bike that had raced in a Giro d'Italia, took it beaming ear to ear. Open and affable, Arturo told us about his racing days.

He grew up in a loving family of eleven children. He was twenty after the war In 1946 when he bought his first bicycle, secondhand, with no gears. He started to race, winning his first eleven races and the winner's jersey for the region. Soon he found a sponsor and became *professionista*. He was so unsophisticated and untraveled that, he told us, already the champion for the region, he was among the leaders in a big race from Trento to Trieste without having the faintest idea which direction Trieste was from Trento.

He acquired an Atalya bicycle with the original, two-lever Campagnolo *cambio*, the hottest gear of the day. With this arrangement, he said, you couldn't change gears on a hill. You had to do it on the flat because you had to pedal backward and simultaneously reach down and move a lever to change into the one other gear. The bicycles were heavy and rugged, with bigger, heavier rims and tires.

He told us it wasn't unusual for a race to last from nine in the morning until six in the evening, often in rain and mud. The races were always out in the country. Few country roads in Italy were paved then. One time, only fifty meters from the finish line in a race, a child trying to help him caused him to fall, and he tumbled head over bike and slid on his belly in the mud over the finish line.

After 1952 he had full-time sponsors. Bartoli and Coppi, the great heroes and legends of Italian bicycle racing, were his friends, and he rode with them in many races. He said he always received energy from the spectators, who cheered him on in the big races. At that time only two or three hundred racers competed in most races. Always, he said, there was a good camaraderie and honor among them. He said he never had any bad experiences because he only created good experiences.

After 1954 he stopped racing and hung up his bicycle. Never looking back, he moved on to work and creating his own large, happy family. His life was interrupted a few years ago by triple-bypass heart surgery. Now he exuded an infectious joy at being alive, cycling again with his friends. You couldn't be around Arturo without smiling.

The Bum Dope Epiphany

It was late by the time we approached the border into Poland, and we'd already traveled almost a hundred miles. There was an unexpected long climb before the Polish border, where the plains met the foothills of the Carpathian Mountains. The road climbed straight at six percent or more for at least a mile, above which the road was hidden in ever-higher passes blanketed in forest.

As it came into view, my heart sank. Just looking at it seemed to make my legs weaker. I tried to remember what Luigi had told me about not "seeing" the hills, but I could feel the discouragement creeping into my legs.

Nino said, "It doesn't look too bad—can't be more than a mile." Rolling my eyes under my glasses, I gazed up at the climb, estimating it would go on for several miles. *Bum dope Nino strikes again.* I chuckled to myself, remembering the revelation that suddenly explained the "bum dope" phenomenon.

I'd begun to think he must be hard of hearing, and worried about how I could tactfully suggest he get a hearing test. Then I began to notice that he answered the questions of the men with painstaking accuracy and precision, in contrast to the offhand way he'd toss off answers to mine.

The revelation came the other day after listening to his conversation with Bruno; his answers to Bruno's questions were detailed and precise.

It finally dawned on me: *Omygawd, he isn't hard of hearing—he just doesn't listen to women!* He'd get the gist of it when a woman was speaking, but he'd tune out the details.

Raised in a family where I'd been listened to and treated with respect all my life, I'd heard of men who didn't listen to women, but I'd never actually met one—at least not one so blatant that I could recognize it. I laughed out loud at how preposterous and obvious it suddenly became. Of course! That was it! I couldn't believe it took me this long to figure it out. So deeply was this attitude ingrained in his psyche that I was sure he wasn't consciously aware of it; wouldn't listen, hear, or believe me if I told him, and would be mad as hell besides.

Another piece to the puzzle fell into place. In addition to not listening to women, it was important for him to be the authority figure, to have the answer for any question "the little woman" would ask. So, if he hadn't heard the whole question or didn't know the answer, he'd just give it his best guess, or actually make something up. It was from this strategy that all the "bum dope" occurred. He'd even tell me how far it was to somewhere he'd never been when he had no map.

I liked men. I respected men. I just didn't consider myself to be less than them, and I certainly expected to be heard when I had something to say. Head of my little family since I was divorced in my twenties, I'd married again, and once laughed at my husband because he'd suggested I ask his permission to buy a dress with my own money. I did not subjugate well, and my resistance to the male power ethic became stronger as I got older. *Well, save your energy, you're not going to change Nino,* I told myself, turning my thoughts to the climb.

Poland by Almost the Right Route

I made my way up slowly with Dottore, Nino, and a few others. Occasionally I'd catch a glance from Dottore's canny blue eyes, each of us offering silent support to the other.

At the top of the miles-long climb, a few of the men smiled and gave me the thumbs-up as I rolled into the rest stop. Increasingly aware of my growing alienation from Nino, never had I been more grateful for friendship. I walked around with my legs a couple of feet apart due to chafing and the damn saddle sores. Many of the others were doing the same. Dottore retired to one of the vans to nurse his own wounds; a glance through a window of one of the vans caught poor Dottore bent over the seat with his pants down while someone gingerly applied salve to his poor abused rear. With this many hours on the saddle every day, you were only as strong as your weakest body part.

Our next stop was the Polish border, where we were delayed long enough with the red tape of visas and passports for most of us to become cold and grouchy. Shadows were long and stomachs were growling. I had no idea how far we still had to go.

After we crossed into Poland, the whole feeling of the land changed. We were deep in the mountains now, starting another long climb. Poland was perfectly beautiful, the rising mountains and fragrant pine forests a welcome change from the flat plains we'd been pedaling across. I got a second wind, and cycled up into the cool air of the mountains with Dottore and four or five others. The late afternoon wind sang in the tall pines as we pedaled quietly.

I did the best I could. Sometimes that was pretty good, sometimes it wasn't. The men smiled in acknowledgment when I was climbing a hill well, and they smiled in encouragement when I wasn't.

Well into the high country, small, well-tended farms began to appear, giving the Polish countryside a feeling of settled, rural prosperity. The houses were built of wood, unpainted and faded to gray with the patina of age, with freshly painted shutters and gingerbread trim of unique designs. They seemed quite old, probably predating the communist era. The style of the houses and their decorations were different from anything I'd seen before. It never ceased to amaze me how different everything was over each border, as if each country had developed in a vacuum, completely separate from any other country. Unlike in Czechoslovakia, the houses looked well cared for, as if the people had always had a stake in the land and their destinies.

Later I learned that while the rural countryside had been subjugated and collectivized by the communists in Czechoslovakia, small farmers in Poland put up such a fierce resistance that most of them were left alone, the Soviet communists not having the political will to do battle with the entire countryside. So while the urban centers in Poland lived under the yoke of central planning, the people in the countryside were left to pursue their lives with more freedom and flexibility.

Finally over the last passes, we started the long descent with my heart full of this wonderful adventure with these kind, brave men who were my family for this little space in time, while the completely beautiful, strange new country whizzed by as we hurtled downhill at thirty-five miles per hour, the mountain air singing to my spirit.

There was little traffic—almost no cars and only an occasional truck followed by its cloud of black smoke. As the road flattened out, small farms and houses became more numerous. Piles of brown coal had been dumped at intervals beside the road. Occasionally a housewife approached with a basket or wheelbarrow to cart the heavy stuff home. Brown coal is the most polluting of fuels, but that was all they had. Poland had no foreign exchange to spend for heating oil in the countryside.

At an intersection, one of the vans motioned us onto a side road. We wound uphill again through a thick pine forest sheltering occasional country houses. It didn't seem like a through road to anywhere. I was following Dottore, whose face was becoming an alarming red, and who was huffing and puffing mightily. The grim set of his mouth said he was furious about this new climb. We ground uphill, uphill, and uphill, for another mile or so.

Finally realizing we couldn't possibly be going the right way, we turned into the driveway of a large house, where we dismounted and walked around in circles, as the astonished family came out to greet us. The van had directed us to the wrong turnoff, and it was after six. Poor Dottore was so done in and mad that steam was practically coming out of his ears. I plopped down on a rock and wondered dully how I could possibly cycle another kilometer. Maybe I could just stay here with these people. Maybe they could just put me in a box and ship me home.

Our big concern was that it would be dark soon. Our destination that night was a "workers' resort," whatever that was. After much conversation in Polish and Italian, neither side understanding the other and much map pointing, someone figured out where we were probably supposed to be going. We cycled back down the hill, turned back onto the main road for a few miles, and up another huge hill to our final and pray-to-God correct destination. My tears streamed, and I bit my lip to prevent myself from breaking down into sobs; I hurt beyond pain, again. Almost completely depleted, I only made it up the last hill because Luigino pushed me, cajoling me up. *"Lina, Lina, coraggio! Siamo arrivati!"* ("Take courage, we've arrived!") *"Vai! Vai!"* he exhorted. *"La ultima salita!"* ("The last hill!")

At this, several nearby cyclists booed loudly, as we always did now whenever anyone said, *"La ultima salita,"* which we always knew was always a lie.

But there really is one last hill at the end of every day, and this was it. At the door of the inn I collapsed in a blubbering heap. One hundred and sixteen miles. God, why was I doing this? At this point I had no idea.

"Yes, you do," came the small voice.

"Oh, shut up, Angelo, and let me enjoy my misery."

From his perch on my left shoulder, he shrugged nonchalantly. *"Hey, whatever turns you on, kid."*

"Oh, all *right*," I said, gathering up my spirits and my helmet, which I'd pitched into a flower bed.

Dottore and Antonio, normally the best of friends, got into a terrible shouting match in the courtyard, flinging arms and bellowing at each other at the top of their Italian lungs, which was pretty formidable. Dottore was giving Antonio hell for subjecting us (and especially him) to that horrible and useless climb; Antonio, who'd been in charge of the route, was trying to explain how it happened, all at the same time. The trees almost shook. Our normal good humor had fled two or three climbs ago. At least they didn't come to blows. And showers and dinner awaited.

The Workers' Resort

The workers' resort was exactly what you'd expect a workers' resort to look like. Although surrounded by tall pines and meadows of flowers, the state-owned inn was spare, with polished wood floors and cheap furniture, sparsely placed. Our room contained two small beds with hard pads covered with tight white sheets and a small, plain wardrobe, against bare, clean white walls. It had all the appeal of a sanitarium.

A glance in the mirror reminded me it was getting harder and harder to look like a female at night; or perhaps it was just harder to feel it was important, my main priorities by now being food, pedal, bath, food, sleep.

We decided Nino should shower first, since he took a faster shower than I did. I'd been thinking about this shower for the last couple of hours, and I sighed, "Ahhhhh!" with pleasure as the first warm drops hit my skin. "Oh, this is *heaven*," I shouted to Nino, lustily lathering up my hair and body. Just as this chore was completed, the stream of hot water decreased to a trickle and then a dribble... and then nothing. Nothing? I fiddled with the faucets. Obviously most of the men had beat us to the showers, and the hotel had not only run out of hot water but had run out of water, period. I stood there fully lathered, incredulous that God would heap this indignity upon poor little me after 116 miles in the saddle.

"Nino!" I screamed. I heard him drop something as he came rushing in to see what catastrophe had befallen me. "They've run out of water!" He waited fearfully to see what I'd do next. "Nino, dear," I said, spitting soap suds through my teeth, "please go down to the kitchen and get me a bucket of hot water! I'm full of soap!"

"What if they won't give me one?"

"Then screw the cook! I don't care what you have to do! Just get me a bucket of water so I can get this fucking soap off!" My remaining veneer of civilization had fled.

He did. I sat in the tub as he gently poured it over me, ever so slowly, as I rinsed off. I peeked up at him from one soapy eye. He was in his "infinite patience" mode. Poor man—how he suffered.

I tossed down my usual Advil and went to dinner with no makeup, stripped now of any gender identification and ego. Important things had shrunk to food and rest. At dinner, we sat at picnic-style tables for six, with benches. The food was served family style. I took a small serving as the bowl of goulash was passed, thinking I could go back for more. *Big* mistake. The men pounced on the food. I should have noticed the abnormally haunted look of hunger in their eyes. There was no more. The kitchen had calculated exactly how much food fifty normal people would eat, half of whom would be women and children, and that's exactly how much there was. Everyone was still hungry, and there was no bread. I had no idea how I could continue to pedal tomorrow, which would be the longest day of the trip, with so little food. Utterly discouraged, I excused myself and went to bed, where at least I could be warm.

As I propped myself up in bed to read, I heard a commotion outside. Peering out of the window, I saw some of the men raiding the vans for tomorrow's lunch supplies, along with the remaining stashes of wine. Dottore, the other organizers, and the drivers were safely out of earshot, eating at a nearby annex. The men were tiptoeing noisily around as if they were robbing a bank, although I couldn't figure out for whose benefit they were trying to tiptoe, since it was our own stuff. Amid stifled laughter, food and wine was sneaked furtively into the inn. Grumbles in the dining room turned to cheers. As I was contemplating the effort of getting dressed again, Nino came in with a huge sandwich for me and a glass of wine. He didn't say anything. I'd come to know this was normal for him, that his caring just didn't come with words. I took it gratefully, pulling his head down to give him a kiss. I ate in bed, feeling like the queen of Sheba.

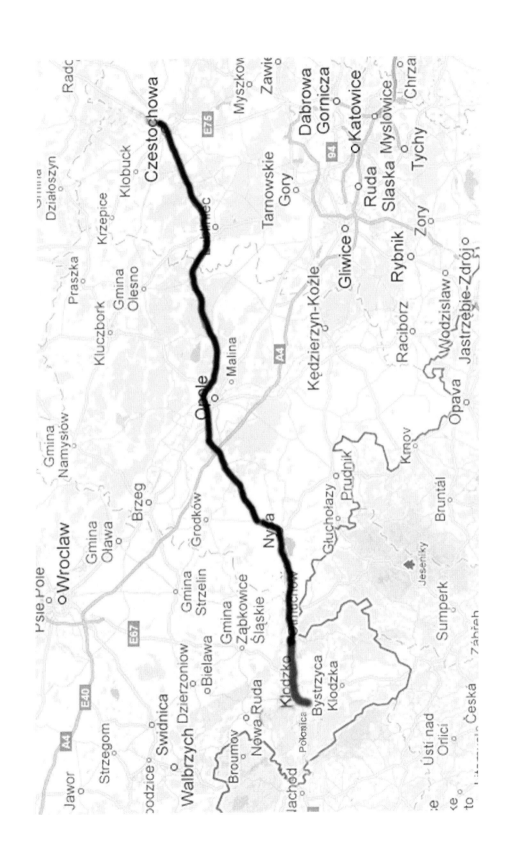

14

Day Eight: Polonica to Czestochowa, 139 miles

I Become Less Popular

I awoke miraculously refreshed; it must have been the sandwich and Nino's kind offer of it, after which I'd drifted off to a contented, deep sleep. Today would be the longest day, projected to be 140 miles. In eastern Europe, these overlong days had been a necessity because that was how far we had to cycle to get to a hotel big enough to accommodate us all, tourist hotels not having been a communist priority. The only way I could deal with the distance we'd have to pedal today was to absolutely avoid thinking about it and proceed as if I would absolutely be able to do it.

We were off by eight in the morning, after an unfortunate incident that made me aware of a slight shift in the general attitude of the men. They enjoyed having me along more, it seemed, when I needed more help and had more trouble keeping up. They were in the habit of asking me, "*Stanca, Lina?*" ("Are you tired?") They enjoyed offering me comfort and sympathy. But when I started to answer, "*No, grazie, sento bene,*" ("No thanks, I feel fine,") they would look surprised and almost a little disappointed; they'd enjoyed having a woman along to take care of.

When Italians say they are departing at eight o'clock, this means you should be mounted up and ready to go by seven-forty-five. This morning I'd arrived at eight and had been accused of being late and holding up the group, even though several cyclists arrived after I did, to no such admonition. *Hmmm.* The message was: "Now that you expect to cycle like a man, don't expect us to cut you any more slack." I'd noticed this shift for the past couple of days, as some of the slower men had openly resented my passing them. I'd tried to do this inconspicuously, but sometimes it was impossible not to pass them trying to maintain my own pace and rhythm—especially when they were coasting down a roller while I was pedaling like hell so I could use the momentum to get up the next one. I, more than they, had to do whatever I could to optimize my strength. And even in my growing fatigue, I was getting stronger.

Also, there was the business of holding my line. Up until a few days ago, it had been a common occurrence for a few of the cyclists (always the same ones) to overtake and cut in front of me in a pace line, which they'd never do to each other without good reason (such as to get out of a vehicle's way). These tended to be the "weekend warrior" cyclists, whom I'd least want to draft. *Oh God, here comes the worst offender.* I decided to let him horn in on someone else for a change and held my line, inches from the rider in front of me. A glance told me he was angry, and I felt a ripple of disapproval go through the cyclists closest to me. Maybe the word had gone around that Lina was getting a little too big for her britches.

This change of attitude wasn't helped when occasionally I'd cycle between groups. The men I passed *really* didn't like that; as my strength increased, my popularity decreased.

I'd mentioned it to Nino. His shrug told me that not only had I correctly discerned this, but that it was normal, I should've expected it, and not to complain.

This morning it was cold and clear. The sky was a brilliant blue, and the waving grasses of hills and distant plains were rich shades of green. Yet the countryside looked so foreign; it must have been the bare wood of the faded village houses with their gingerbread trim and the round domes and tall spires of the village churches, so reminiscent of the East. The domes and spires could be seen dotting the great plain ahead, marking where villages lay. In the distance, thin columns of black smoke spiraled upward from the tall smokestacks of a factory. Except for a few trucks, there was little traffic. Farmers waved as we rushed by, plowing their fields with plows drawn by huge, muscular draft horses. Only occasionally did we see a tractor—idle, no doubt, from lack of fuel or money to buy it. The lean peasants of the Polish countryside always waved and greeted us openly, with big smiles.

How I wished we could stop and visit; if only I could climb into a time capsule and deposit myself with a bottle of good California wine in someone's kitchen. Speaking fluent Polish, as maybe my ancestors had, I would converse with the family for a couple of hours, drink a toast to our new friendship, and return to the pack without anyone ever having missed me.

Search for My Heritage

Cycling through Poland held special significance for me because my mother's people, though ethnic Germans (we were pretty sure), had come from Breslau, once part of Lower Silesia in Germany. After the war, the region had been made part of Poland again, and the name of the city had been changed to Wroclaw. Was Germany or Poland my mother's homeland? How sad that I didn't really know, would never know.

A cousin had traveled to Wroclaw to research our family history, only to find that the town hall where all the records were kept had been bombed into rubble by the Russians during a siege in early 1945. So my family history on my mother's side was forever lost.

I guess I hoped to feel some kinship with the people as I cycled through Poland, but we never stopped long enough for me to have the opportunity. Not having access to my mother's family history made me feel somehow cast adrift, cut off from my past, especially since I was from a country still defining itself, with such a brief history of its own.

Who was I? Travel makes you ask that, even when you don't intend to, or want to. I was constantly making comparisons between myself and the people among whom I found myself, defining who I was and who I was not. I envied the continuity of history, culture, and traditions enjoyed by Europeans. Many Americans lack knowledge of their family history before their ancestors came to America, usually only one, two, or three generations ago. And so, with a blank slate for our own history and traditions, we tend to reinvent ourselves every generation, which is pretty hard on everybody.

At home I had a friend from Poland, an urban intellectual from Warsaw. He knew who he was. A quiet man, he was short, well-built, with blond hair and honest, direct blue eyes framed by small, round-rimmed glasses. His passion was Tai Chi, the philosophy of which interested him as much as the physical art. He spoke beautiful English; he was a man to whom things like that mattered.

He told me this story: He'd been lucky enough not to lose his parents during the war, but like almost everybody else, they lost their home and everything they had to the bombing, which almost completely destroyed Warsaw. But they sat in the rubble, he said, and chipped mortar off bricks—one for the good brick pile; one for the rubble pile; another for the good brick pile. The Polish people are survivors, he told me in his quiet way. "They could try to bomb us into oblivion and we'd rise again, as we always have. So we just sat there until we'd chipped off all the mortar from every usable brick of every bombed-out building, and we rebuilt our city. And we'd do it again."

I'd be proud to have come from people like that. I'd be proud to have come from Polish people, or from German people. I just wished I knew which it really was.

One thing was for sure. In all the world, I was on the cutting edge, as a woman, of opportunity to become all that I could become. I'd lived in the Middle East and traveled in India and Asia, where I'd been appalled at the condition of women's (and everyone else's) lives. As an American woman, I was more free and had more options in life, along with the cultural sanction to exercise them, than any other women in the world. I was always deeply conscious of this fact, and deeply grateful. America is the expression of the great experiment of freedom, the opportunity to grow toward your highest and best self—or not. Disorderly, chaotic, sometimes greedy, and often unfair, America at least tries to get it right. It is enormously exciting to have been born an American woman, and I wouldn't trade it for anything.

Finally we pulled over for the first rest stop, at sixty kilometers. It was too long between rest stops, but I knew how far we had to go today. As the food was being set out, cyclists rummaged in the vans for their rain gear. An upward glance revealed an ominously darkening sky. As I suited up for the rain, my tired legs told me I'd better not stop for any reason today. Even though I was getting stronger, my fatigue was increasing every day, too. A nagging reality was pounding on my door, the way you'd feel writing checks when you knew you had no money in the bank. If I let myself think about it, I'd be down for the count. I focused on getting a *panino*.

I loved the hustle and bustle of our rest stops, the commotion of getting us fed amid the mellifluous Italian chatter. As usual, Antonio was giving directions, people were waiting on Dottore, guys were peeing in the bushes, Ciccio was doing sit-ups, and cyclists were standing in line at the meat cutter for meat and cheese for their rolls, dispensed by the cheerful wives.

Today we had bananas, a real treat. Fresh fruit had become harder to come by, since there were few markets as well as few fruit crops the farther we penetrated into Eastern Europe. Also, it was becoming harder for the women in charge of procuring our food to find enough bread for our group; sometimes village bakeries didn't have enough surplus to sell us all we needed.

It amused me how my perspective toward food had changed. The unadorned bread, meat, and cheese now seemed to me an incredible feast. The lean bodies and unmechanized farms of the local farm people betrayed that they had few luxuries, and probably little meat. A luxury here would be a full stomach in every season.

The Sports Aids

Back on the bikes. The pace lines were fast and steady, the rhythm hypnotic. The countryside was big, wide, and sparsely populated. This was really freedom, where we could stretch out our spirits as far as we wanted. It was rare, in the America I knew, to have enough time to really think deeply on a subject, to think about it until you were truly finished thinking about it. Reveling in the freedom of the open road and the space and time to think, I reflected on my passion for cycling. This passion had reached deep within me. I saw it as a collage within which I pedaled my bicycle freely, fast, strong, and steady, along roads bisecting enormous open plains with wild waving grasses, feeling the wind in every pore, aware of the sound and the quality of the wind, the strength in my legs creating the speed, my body working in harmony with the bicycle—one with it—like a well-oiled machine, the view for miles ahead over the open, undulating plains to blue mountains in the distance, the gathering thunderclouds overhead with their palpable, imminent threat—all this made me feel a depth of aliveness I'd never felt before, through to the core of my soul. This was my life now, and there was no other.

It got colder, and it rained. It let up, and a giant rainbow spanned the horizon. Then it rained again. Another sixty kilometers, another rest stop. This should have been toward the end of our day, but it wasn't. *Can't be so damn tired yet—I'll make it—oh right, and we'll be in Moscow in time for dinner—No! I'll make it.* But denial as a survival tool was beginning to appear ridiculous even to me. Food. Focus on food.

Dottore, Nino, and the support people had gone into a small restaurant for soup, while the cyclists ate *panini* and huddled by the van brewing the espresso, under a dripping tree. I joined the cyclists, drawn by Luigi's presence and the steamy rich aroma of the espresso. Some of us, including me, were shaking with the cold. Someone brought out a bottle of grappa. Espresso was poured, and everyone was offered a shot of grappa for their espresso. My good judgment was easily seduced by my desire to be warm inside, if not outside, as I offered my cup. And again. Before I thought about it, I'd had three espressos and three shots of grappa. Then it was time to go. I was still hungry, so I fished a solid bar of dark chocolate I'd been saving out of my bike pack, and ate it.

Soon we were on the road. After about fifteen minutes, the most amazing thing happened. Suddenly and seemingly without effort, I took off like I was shot out of a cannon. "Whoa!" I said aloud, utterly astounded. "How can these be my legs? I can't possibly go this fast!" I looked down at my legs, moving like pistons, as if they belonged to a stranger.

"Angelo! What on earth is this?"

He was laughing. "*Hey, think about it, kid; you'll figure it out.*"

Omygawd. Of course. The espresso, the grappa, and the chocolate had all kicked in at the same time. I was turbo-charged. I passed many of the cyclists; I couldn't help myself. I was drunk with power. I wished Nino were here, so I could—*Hah!*—leave him in the dust. *Gawdalmighty, they ought to bottle this stuff!* Then I threw back my head and laughed, realizing that "this stuff" was already available in many forms—none of them, however, legal.

I milked it for all it was worth, knowing it would probably never happen again; but after an hour or so the inevitable blood-sugar crash happened, and I began to come down. I slowed down as I came down. Pretty soon the men were passing me again, giving me curious looks. How could I explain? Soon my fellow imbibers passed, laughing. "*Eh, Lina, troppo grappa? Troppo espresso?*" ("Hey, Lina, too much grappa? Too much espresso?") Bruno, my pious friend, passed, tsk-tsking and shaking his finger at me. Lord, I'd never live it down.

By now I had a headache and I wasn't feeling too hot, and we still had a long way to go. Dottore finally caught up with me, the question in his eyes asking why it had taken him so long to catch up with me. "I started earlier," I lied, knowing he hadn't seen my bionic woman stunt. Sheepishly I slipped in behind him, nursing my early hangover.

I reflected that of the two, the espresso-grappa-chocolate special and the shot to my spirit from the freedom of cycling the great open roads of the world, I'd still take the latter any time.

Longest Day

When things are only a little tough, you can complain with impunity. But when things really get tough, no one complains; you can't afford to waste the energy, needed for the task at hand. It was dinnertime, we were still pedaling, and I still didn't know how far we had to go. "*Dottore, quanto lontano e Czestochowa?*" ("How far is Czestochowa?")

"*Non lo so. Spero presto. Stanca?*" ("I don't know. I hope soon. Are you tired?")

"*Sì.*" And tired wasn't the half of it. My head throbbed. I shifted painfully on my seat, trying to avoid sitting directly on the saddle sores. I glanced over at Dottore's ample rear, hoping his padding was letting him fare better than I was. Luigi and Luigino had showed me how to rest one leg at a time by standing and gliding first on one pedal, than the other. But now my feet hurt too much to do even that—to say nothing of my neck, shoulders, back, and hands. I glanced around at the men; many were in the same boat, shifting gingerly around, looking for the least painful position for their derrieres.

It was becoming dark. We'd been on the road for twelve hours, including our stops. A quiet fell over the group. I pedaled through my hangover and even got a second wind around eight thirty, as the last of the light faded. *Amazing. Women don't know what they're capable of*, I thought.

At last we could see the glow of Czestochowa in the sky, and soon we were pedaling through the outskirts of town. These were the longest outskirts I'd ever pedaled. The darkness seemed to take away my groundedness and my sense of time. I was lightheaded, and I fought off a feeling that I was floating, knowing it was dangerous, knowing I needed to keep grounded. We pedaled and pedaled until I was sure we'd spend the whole night circling the town, knowing I'd dream of circling the town, that the dream wouldn't be so far from the reality.

At the hotel, we stored our bicycles in the boiler room, letting some air out of our tires so they wouldn't blow out in the hot room. It was nine thirty. The 139 miles we'd covered today was much farther than most of us had ever pedaled in a day. Two guys fell down as they got off their bikes. We stumbled around in a happy, self-satisfied daze, congratulating each other, "*Complimenti! Complimenti!*"

While we waited for dinner, Dottore told me that in his opinion, cycling required more strength of character than any other sport, and he thought I had great strength of character. "*Anche lei,*" ("And you too,") I said. I was surprised that he looked surprised at my reply. Perhaps it was normal, in the Italian perception, for a man to have strength of character, but not for a woman? How little I knew about these people; I was beginning to get glimpses of the complexity of the Italian character. Someday, when I could speak good Italian, I'd really be able to talk to Dottore, to know what he was really like behind his public persona.

Nino and I fell into a mode of old friends who had been through a lot together, grateful for each other's company and too weary to discuss our differences. Each of us respected the other's survival, which had become our mutual focus for the rest of the trip.

At dinner, the first course was clear broth. Oh God, we weren't going to get enough to eat again. I opined to the table, "*Eh, di nuovo, zuppa non chiaro sul concetto.*" Nino grimaced as the crack made the rounds to weary chuckles at my pathetic attempts at their language; but I bet no one would ever be able to look at clear broth again without remembering "unclear-on-the-concept soup."

15

Day Nine: Czestochowa to Lodz, 80 miles

The Black Madonna

We set off late for the monastery at Jasna Gora, where pilgrims from all over Christendom had been coming for six hundred years to pour out their sorrows and pray for miracles at the picture of the Black Madonna, called Our Lady of Czestochowa. The picture's origins are a mystery, but stories of miracles associated with it have been passed down through time ever since a Polish duke gave the picture to the monastery in 1384, after having been told to do so in a dream. Since then, the monastery had survived the winds of change in war, siege, fire, shifts of borders and power. But things Polish persevere. The monastery has been the home of the Pauline order of monks since its beginning in the fourteenth century.

We pedaled to the monastery where we congregated in a large stone outer courtyard while we waited for someone who would guide us to see the monastery and its treasures, and the famous Black Madonna. A few cyclists were trying to shush the group, amid our normal noise and commotion. Finally we quieted down enough for

Dottore to tell us he'd arranged for an Italian-speaking monk to be our guide, and to be quiet and behave ourselves.

Nino told me that as a woman (I'd almost forgotten), I couldn't enter without a skirt, so I dove into the luggage van and hurriedly fished one out of my bag to slip over my bike shorts.

Our guide was a tall and lanky young monk, not more than thirty. He was Italian and had the widest grin I'd ever seen, so happy was he to see his countrymen and to speak his native tongue. He told us he used to be a cyclist and how much he missed cycling. His white monk's robes swept the ground as he admired our beautiful bicycles, forgetting for the moment he was a monk, and was supposed to have renounced such extravagant pleasures. Dottore and Antonio exchanged glances; I wondered if they were thinking what I hoped they were thinking.

The stone monastery had a dark splendor about it, its lofty, spacious halls filled with mystery, the patina of age, and glorious art. The young priest showed us through the museum rooms, leading us finally to the Black Madonna picture itself, cloistered in a small inner sanctuary behind an elaborate altar. The picture, the monk told us, may date back as far as the sixth century. The skin of the Madonna and Child is a dark tawny to black, and the original painting, now in an elaborate frame, was overlaid at a later time with silver ornamentation and a crown. A sacredness transcending all religions emanated from the faces of the Madonna and Child. I was awed by the mystery of it in this Catholic monastery from which I was philosophically so separate, yet joined in spirit. We filed past as quietly as we could, our cleats clicking softly on the stone floors. Other monks, all young, were seated in the small room, praying before the Black Madonna.

Why was she painted black? Had she really shed tears, as they said? Were the miracles real? We'd never know. Life is full of miracles and mysteries.

A New Dream for the Monk

As we returned to the monastery courtyard and our bikes, an excited buzz was going around in the group. My suspicion was confirmed! It had been decided that we'd give the bicycle intended for President Vaclav Havel of Czechoslovakia, instead, to the monk.

We formed a circle around him in the courtyard, and Dottore stepped forward to make the gift and a little speech. The young monk's astonished eyes grew large, and his smile spread from ear to ear. He was struck speechless, and just stood there in his white robes, grinning helplessly. Someone had wheeled the bicycle out of its place of honor in the van, and into the circle. The sun glinted off the metallic, sky blue paint, and shone off the Campagnolo components and the silver letters that said "De Rosa" on the frame. He hiked up his robes and mounted it, his experienced hands

The Monk's Impossible Dream

caressing the brake hoods. There wasn't a dry eye in the house.

Amid applause and furtive sniffles, Antonio presented him with the whole outfit to go with the bicycle: shorts, Italian jersey, cap, cleats. Nino, always the cynic, whispered, "He'll probably sell it, quit the priesthood, buy a farm, and get married." "Nino!" I chided. "How could you say such a thing?"

But I always wondered how that bicycle affected the monk's life after we left. Would the church hierarchy let him keep it? Surely he wouldn't sell it—would he? Would he ride it, filling his spirit with the wind? Would he sell it and use the money to feed the poor? To find another life? Would he place his cleats reverently next to his rosary, where no one could see? Hey, the God I believe in would understand.

Luigi's Secret

Mounted up once again, I heeded Dottore's glance and slipped into place behind him, since I wasn't up to dealing with anyone's disapproval today. Even after a full night's sleep, I was more tired than ever. The talk at breakfast told me that so were many of the others. We needed a rest day, but we weren't going to get one. However, the eighty miles we'd cover today would seem like a picnic after the last two days, and I'd heard we had no mountains to cross today.

The country was as promised: flat with gentle hills, open plains, small farms, and an occasional village. I let myself be mesmerized by the pace lines, feeling not an individual but a cog in an ever-moving wheel. The peace of it settled over me, and I relaxed into the day.

The pace seemed slower today; either that, or I'd become more accustomed to it. How good it felt to pedal without the anxiety that I wouldn't be able to keep up. I fell back to visit with some of the others—sort of like table-hopping on a bicycle.

After awhile I fell back to cycle alone. Startled by a huge clap of thunder, I pedaled forward again to ride beside Bruno. Huge drops began to plop off the pavement, and pretty soon the sky opened up and soaked us again. We laughed—what else was there to do?

Bruno and I had exhausted all small talk. Now we tried to exchange ideas, but our limited vocabularies in each other's language prevented this, so we pedaled in silence.

I kept thinking about Luigi, and the mystery surrounding him. I had to know. "Bruno, do you know why Luigi quit racing?"

"No," he said, "no one knows." Luigi was cycling just ahead.

I said to Bruno, "I'm going to ask him. Will you translate for me?" Bruno's reluctance showed on his face. "Please?" I entreated, motioning him to ride forward with me.

We pulled up beside Luigi. Bruno glanced at me, and I knew I was imposing on our friendship. Addressing Luigi, he translated as I spoke: "Luigi," I said, summoning up my nerve, "I understand you quit racing when you were winning." He glanced over at me, eyebrows raised in surprise that I knew this. "Why did you quit?" His slow smile told me he'd been asked that question many times before. My intuition told me if my question had come from anyone but Bruno, whose quiet caring was known to everyone, Luigi probably wouldn't have answered.

It seemed like a long time passed before he answered. "I've never told anyone before," he said. "The answer is so simple that no one would have believed me, so I kept it to myself. The competition, and all the politics that go with it, was destroying my love for the sport. For me, winning was empty without passion. The love of the sport was the most important to me, so I gave up the racing career and kept the passion."

A wave of emotion, a respect for him and a sharing of that passion, washed over me. I loved the direction of his will, the focused determination of his individuality, cutting like a knife through the extraneous stuff of life. No matter what they said about him, or what more there was to his story, he'd charted his own course.

Bruno said, "Ah-h-h," understanding.

My hand flew to my heart. "*Capisco, Luigi. Grazie.*" ("I understand, Luigi. Thanks.") Of course. It fit perfectly with what I intuitively knew about him. He was simply his own man.

"Tell me, Luigi," I continued through Bruno, "after all these years, do you still feel such a strong passion for cycling?"

"*Si*," he said, "it's just as strong now as before. The thrill for me has always been the power when I'm climbing, and the speed, and the freedom. And you?" he asked.

With Bruno's help I tried to put it in Italian, so I could talk to him directly. "For me it is the combination of so many things that I love—the speed, the wind, the pedaling, the open country, the exploring, the freedom, being one with the bicycle."

He looked at me with a long slow smile that welcomed my knowledge of him, and his of me. We were saved from the awkwardness of the revealing moment by Luigi's friends, who rode up from the rear, sweeping Luigi ahead with them.

I thanked Bruno and asked him to sit with us at dinner tonight, hoping Nino would help with our conversation.

At the rest stop I excused myself from Nino, who was busy chatting with Dottore. I sat on an old rock wall and munched my *panino*, happy not to make conversation and just sit quietly. Nino and I spent less and less time together now during the rest stops. Continuing to ignore the fingers of fatigue and weakness trying to creep up my legs couldn't hold it at bay for much longer. I'd programmed myself for ten days, and tomorrow was the last day. Closing my eyes, I thanked God I'd made it this far, and asked strength for one more day.

Seeing the fatigue that must have showed on my face, Luciana brought me an apple, Umberto put some honey into my water bottle, Bruno brought me an espresso, and Maria Pia slipped me a secret chocolate bar she'd been saving. Bless them; these kindnesses had helped get me this far and would help get me through this day, too. Italians really do say, "*Mangia! Mangia!*" ("Eat! Do eat!") So I stuffed the calories down, fuel for the car, looking forward to the day when I'd look forward to a meal again.

The Accident

By mid-afternoon we entered Lodz, an industrial city. Cobblestones again. Dangerous cobblestones, like in Prague; big stones, old and broken, bisected everywhere by odd-angled trolley tracks. It was pay-attention time, trying to keep my front wheel from slipping in between the track and the cobblestones, like it had in Prague. Crossing tracks while riding in a group is always risky business, with so little room to maneuver. We tended to bunch up at such spots, slowing down to where our wheels wobbled. Sometimes someone stopped, causing everybody in back to stop. My eyes were glued to the tracks as I tried to cross while keeping a little distance from the others, when I heard a great commotion to the rear. Someone had fallen on the tracks.

Somebody had stopped abruptly, I heard, causing Sergio to fall. Sergio was an older man, retired, and a good rider. He couldn't get up, and it was feared he had a broken leg. We all milled around while Dottore and Francesco called an ambulance. It was decided that the rest of us should proceed to the hotel.

Sobered by the injury of one of our own, we picked our way gingerly across town to the Grand Hotel, which was anything but grand.

Lodz

The thing that struck me first about Lodz was the soot. Most of the buildings were black with soot from the smokestacks of coal-fired industry, giving the city the look of the industrial era of the nineteenth century, which wasn't far off the mark.

Lodz, a city of just under a million, belonged to the Russians before World War I, who developed it from a small village into a large industrial city, producing mostly textiles. Germans occupied it next, but the Poles reclaimed it in 1918, after fierce fighting.

It was occupied again by Hitler's Nazi armies in World War II, who laid siege to the city's Jewish ghettos. Poland had an enormous Jewish population before the Nazi onslaught. A few escaped, but those who hadn't been shipped off to the death camps were killed or died of disease or starvation in the sealed-off ghettos during the war. It was a horror almost too great to comprehend.

The city's bleak appearance reflected its tragic history, but the faces of people on the streets were full of purpose, full of hope. I remembered again my Polish guest who told me that Poles would always survive and rebuild their country, no matter what tragic hand history dealt them. In terms relative to history, these were good times. The Iron Curtain had lifted, along with hopes, expectations, and, I noticed, an influx of Japanese businessmen with briefcases. Poland's transition to a democratic society would be fraught with hardship and difficulties, but it would be a whole lot better than the alternatives of the recent past. Poles were betting their lives on it. Against that panorama, the soot didn't seem so important.

The Italians were very unhappy with our hotel, which was large, sooty, seedy, and across the tracks from the ugly railroad station. The old and shabby rooms had no baths and no one could find the showers, which turned out to be located on alternate floors. Soon the hotel was filled with loud Italian men wrapped only in scanty towels, running up and down hallways looking for the showers.

Nino, ever resourceful, did a secret reconnaissance and discovered a shower no one had found on the first floor. We sneaked down the stairs hoping no one would see us, towels hidden under our clean clothes. The tub handles creaked and the pipes groaned, but they produced a blissful stream of hot water under which I stood for a long time, having convinced myself *hey, I deserve this.*

At dinner Dottore gave us the sad news about Sergio: he had a broken femur and internal bleeding, which would require surgery within forty-eight hours. Dottore and Francesco had followed the ambulance to the hospital in one of the vans. Dottore said he was shocked at how dirty the hospital was, and at the primitive facilities. They would never allow a member of the group to stay there, he said, much less to undergo surgery. So they sent for a private jet from Italy to pick him up. Dottore would ride with Sergio tomorrow in the ambulance to Warsaw, where the plane would be waiting.

Dinner was unusually subdued, each of us facing, unspoken, our vulnerability, our mortality on a bicycle, and the hazards of cycling in countries lacking in modern facilities. Was an accident, assuming the exercise of attention and reasonable caution, just the luck of the draw? I thought about the interplay of karma, chance, and diligence, which would remain forever a mystery to me. You take a lot of stuff for granted hopping around the world on a bicycle. Well, they call that faith. We all knew that.

We dined in the hotel's ballroom. Like other places we'd stayed, it recalled a more elegant past, in better times. Gothic arches of imposing height soared above us, and the walls were decorated with friezes set off by yellow, white, and gold gilt paint, peeling a little at the edges. Chandeliers softly illuminated the intricate wood inlays of the parquet floors and the white linen and silver table service. The once-fine linen was patched here and there, and pieces in the parquet floors were shriveled in places with age. A priceless medieval tapestry, two stories high, covered much of one wall, and a perfectly terrible band made up of long-haired youths in bellbottoms played, aptly, "Help Me Make It Through the Night."

We needed the music tonight, and Dottore whisked me out to the dance floor. Hardly anyone danced, the wives and I being the only women present, but everyone was grateful for the music to lighten our spirits. Glancing wistfully over to the tables where the men sat, I wished I could dance with them, not daring to think about dancing with Luigi. But Nino had a way of being very possessive without actually seeming so, and the men respected that.

After dinner some of us retired to the salon bar to view and be viewed by the local cognoscenti. The men and women in the bar were mostly young, good-looking and slender, most with dark hair and milk-white skin, giving them a slightly malnourished look. Some men and women were dressed in business attire, carrying briefcases— the new entrepreneurs of Lodz. A few women were wearing party dresses, and all the men were wearing suits. They were trying to emulate western fashion, but their clothes were of poor quality. They were all serious, and engaged in intense conversation. Having read that Poland has always had a rich intellectual life, I wished I could've listened in on one of the conversations going on around me.

By tomorrow night we'd be in Warsaw. It had been a great adventure, but it seemed like it had been going on forever, as if we had no other life. In a relaxed mood, Nino and I drank a toast to the likelihood of making it to Warsaw without killing each other, which, as it turned out, was a little premature.

"You're tough, Lina," he said.

"No tougher than you," I rejoined.

We clinked glasses, finished off the cognac, and dragged ourselves up the wide, creaking wood stairs to bed.

I lay awake for a long time, my mind filled with too many images to sleep. I looked over at Nino, now sleeping peacefully. Unlike me, he didn't seem much affected by events; or if he was, he never showed it. An intentional stranger, he asked to be known only for how he chose to appear. Operating from hidden agendas was his natural mode of being. We would always have a bond after what we'd shared, yet I knew little of how he really felt.

On rare nights after too much wine, he'd hinted at deeply buried fears and regrets: a death fear that gripped his gut on the battlefield; a grief that would never abate at the death of his wife and a son; and a deep-seated, superstitious fear from his ancient Italian roots of a curse put upon him by the village girl he didn't marry. But as soon as he realized he was giving voice to these things, he'd quickly change the subject.

Culturally, he was no longer pure Italian; he'd adopted too many American values. Neither would he ever be a true cultural American. He was bicultural—a state of wider experience, with loneliness and isolation on the flip side. This, with his intentional impassivity, kept me from him, which he intended, and which was just as well. As he slept, I looked at him with a sudden ache in my heart for what might have been. I put my arm around him, and the pillow grew damp with my tears.

I'd wanted to know him, but I never would.

Our group at Czestochowa

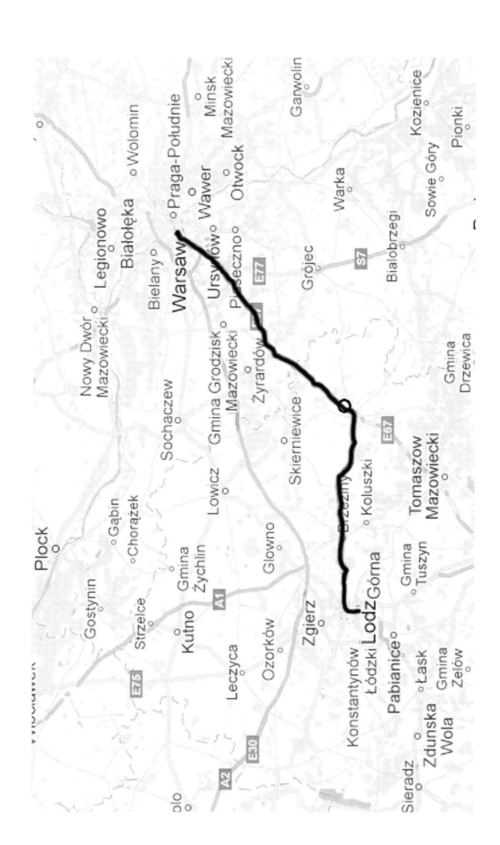

16

Day Ten: Lodz to Warsaw, 85 miles

Last Day

I awoke filled with a sense of gratitude at having made it this far, mixed with the gnawing-at-my-gut fear I'd refused to name: that I couldn't hold out through this one more, last day. Closing my eyes, I visualized portioning out to myself my tenth day's supply of energy and strength, bundles of it, little stars of light going into me along the route—sort of like God's time-release vitamin—and pictured myself pedaling with the pack triumphantly through the streets of downtown Warsaw.

Today would be a shorter day. I smiled; at home I'd consider pedaling eighty-five miles anything but a short day. But the pedaling was supposed to be flat today, and this afternoon we'd be in Warsaw.

On the road, the land again was a vast, endless expanse of green, undulating almost imperceptibly. The pace lines were quiet and fast. Even Dottore was going like a house afire; the horse-to-the-barn syndrome was in full swing. I was more tired than I thought; the cumulative fatigue was biting at my heels.

God, I can't keep up. Got to. Got to get eighty-five miles out of my legs today. So god-awful tired. "Angelo?" Nothing. "Thanks a lot, Mr. No Comment." Taking a long pull on my water bottle, I gripped the handlebars, put my head down, and pushed harder and faster, trying to overpower the doubt creeping in that I could actually make the eighty-five miles today. The ever-present knowledge that I'd collapse before I'd quit didn't scare me anymore. It just was. Anyway, I was too tired to be scared. *Please, God, don't let me collapse.*

Angelo suddenly appeared, lounging as usual on my left shoulder, "*Hey, Ms. Dying Heroine, cut the drama and relax; it'll conserve your energy. It's practically a done deal, kid; just keep pedaling for a few more hours.*"

"Easy for you to say. Oh, okay." I dropped back to pedal beside Francesco, biting my lip. He looked over at me and slowed just a little. I nodded my thanks.

We Entertain the Farmers

The van folks scouted ahead and got a farmer's permission to set up our rest stop in a field beside his orchard. The normal hullabaloo of our rest stop was great entertainment for the neighbors. A farm family across the street brought out chairs, which they set beside the road. They even propped up the baby—resplendent in a pink knitted hat with a wide brim—against the side of her wicker pram, so she, too, could see. Then they seated themselves—father, mother, girl, boy, and baby, all in a row, to watch the show. They all sat with their right legs crossed over their left, with almost identical, perfectly round peasant faces, sandy hair, fair skin, and bright rosy cheeks. I wasn't sure what about us was so entertaining, unless it was our normal Italian flamboyance, but no movie audience was ever more rapt.

Meanwhile, our host milked his cow for us on the spot. The fresh milk right out of the cow was like ambrosia in the espresso. The farmer's daughter presented us with fresh eggs she'd just collected.

Then they, too, stood at the sidelines and watched, fascinated, while we laughed and joked, shouted greetings, drank wine or fussed with our bicycles, and Ciccio did his usual sit-ups and munched on cloves of garlic. "Good for the blood," he always said, pounding his chest. We invited the family to join us for *panini*, but they were shy and preferred to remain on the sidelines. They were reluctant to accept even the bottle of wine we offered, until we convinced them we had plenty and that it was a gift from our heart.

Strolling around, I watched the men lounging in the grass and the farm families watching us, and tried to ignore my various hurting body parts. I was afraid if I sat down I wouldn't be able to get up again. I ate, not wanting any of it, and drank three espressos. Where was my energy? Jogging in place for a couple of minutes, I tried to whip it up. *C'mon,* I told myself, *only another fifty flat miles.*

I'd become invisible to the men. No longer the woman to cherish and take care of, I was just another cyclist. This was what I wanted, wasn't it? Yes, but… it didn't feel right. I missed the I-am-woman-you-are-man feeling. I felt again the undercurrent of resentment from some of them for stepping out of my expected role, for doing what they did, for being as strong on the bike now as some of the men. Nino was nowhere to be seen, not cottoning much to Lina the cyclist. I sighed. Well, so be it. Finding Bruno, I sat down beside him and then stretched out in the warm grass.

Suddenly someone shook my shoulder, and I wakened with a start. "*Lina, ti sveglia!*" ("Lina, wake up!") I'd had no intention of dozing off. The last group was getting ready to shove off, so I jumped to my feet and, half conscious, scrambled onto my bicycle.

I Get Left

We hadn't been on the road again for long when the three espressos took their toll, and I had to make a stop. I started off again, off the back and alone now but unconcerned; I'd catch up soon enough, as I had before. I enjoyed pedaling lazily at my own pace for a few minutes, but soon realized I'd better step it up to catch up to the group.

Ten or fifteen minutes went by without catching sight of them. I began to feel a little uneasy. A village appeared, where I could have turned any of several different directions. There were no signs. Surely someone will wait for me here, to be sure I don't take a wrong turn. But no one was waiting, and I began to feel strangely disconnected. I stopped and asked, "Warsaw?" People pointed. I followed their fingers.

Pedaling away from the village, I tried to make sense of the situation. This might not have been so unusual in an American group, where people were more independent, and maverick individuals sometimes went off in their own directions. But in an Italian group, the cyclists identified less as individuals and more as members of the group. Normally it wouldn't take more than a few minutes for someone in the group to realize someone was missing, and soon they'd stop and wait. Was it possible no one had noticed I was missing? Where was Nino, and where was Bruno, who usually waited? *Surely Nino will eventually wait for me*, I reassured myself. I tried to relax, to enjoy the countryside and the day, but over some rollers I could see long stretches ahead, and the group was nowhere in sight.

I thought I was pedaling a little faster than the slowest group, but a glance at my cyclometer told me that actually I was going probably a little slower than these cyclists, who would be traveling faster in pace lines. My fatigue was slowing me down. It was going on half an hour now. No one would not be missed or would be allowed to be off the back for that long. My God, it wasn't possible they'd just left me, was it? *No, of course not; my nerves are clouding my thinking.* But what other explanation was there?

Now I looked for Nino or someone over each roller, but the country was empty. Soon I pedaled through another small town. Again, there were several turns I could've taken, but only one would be the right one. I queried people on the sidewalks, "Warsaw?" Again they pointed, and I followed. With every juncture in the road now, I knew my chances of making a mistake increased. "Angelo, help me!"

"*So far, so good, kid,*" he said. "*But turn on all your homing beacons. It looks like you're on your own.*"

The realization sunk in; they really had left me. How could this be? Well, it was. What if they never waited, and I never caught up? What if every group thought I was pedaling with some other group? What if they didn't think about it at all? What if they thought, *If she wants to cycle like a man, let her fend for herself like a man?* But they would never do this to one of their own men, and as for Nino... a flash of rage told me I'd better just concentrate at the task at hand now, and deal with my feelings later.

I'd been out here alone for over an hour, and had no idea where I was. I hadn't seen any road signs, which made me wonder if I really was going the right way. The gray skies obscured the sun, preventing me from knowing even the direction I was heading. If I was on the road to Warsaw, I'd be heading northeast. I tried to calm myself, thinking surely this will all work out. Never under any circumstances, I vowed, would I ever again cycle in unfamiliar country without a map and compass in my possession.

Cycling through a wooded area, I flinched at volleys of gunshots, very close to the road. Hunters? Military maneuvers? I hadn't seen a newspaper in awhile; was there some conflict here? I peered into the trees, seeing nothing, fighting down the little knot of fear in my stomach. Now I prayed to see Nino over each rise.

Suppose I never found them? I didn't know if there would be another rest stop. Suppose I had to find my way all the way to Warsaw, and I never found them? My sense told me I was probably on the right road. If not, I'd stay at a farm tonight, or at worst, I could sleep hidden in the forest.

I took stock: I had a Power Bar and almost a full double water bottle. Like a fool, I'd left the itinerary with the name of the hotel in my bag, which was in one of the vans along with my clothes, travelers checks, and map. Warsaw was a city of three million people, and the likelihood of finding the group would be pretty low. I supposed I could ask someone at a hotel to check other hotels, but as my tears flowed, I knew I really didn't want to see them again, these people I thought were my friends. My mind darted around. Thank God I had my jacket on. Mentally I went over the contents of my bike pack: in my wallet I had my passport, visa, two credit cards, and maybe a couple of hundred dollars in Italian lira. Well okay, survival wouldn't be a problem. No, it wasn't okay. I was sick at heart, and the grief wasn't mixing well with the fear, as my stomach churned.

"*Get a grip on yourself!*" admonished Angelo. "*Focus only on getting to Warsaw.*"

"Okay, Angelo, I'll try."

"*Don't give me this 'try' crap. Do it!*"

"Okay, okay." Almost two hours. My aloneness made it seem much longer. I forced myself to think about what I'd do when I got to Warsaw. First, I'd find a hotel that took a credit card. Then I'd find a bank, and try to buy something to wear. I could eat at the hotel on my credit card, and tomorrow—I was too angry and hurt to know if I even wanted to try to find the group—I'd see about buying a train ticket back to Italy and Verona. To hell with them.

By now I was pedaling only twelve or thirteen miles per hour; my discouragement had taken me over, and I just couldn't go any faster. I figured about twenty miles to go. I pedaled on dully, in grim acceptance of my situation. Abandonment was a new experience for me. Another town, this one more like a suburb. "Warsaw?" Again I followed their pointed fingers.

The Volcano Erupts

A flood of relief came over me to see a road sign proclaiming, "Warsaw 20 kilometers." Soon I spotted one of our vans coming toward me. Antonio screeched to a halt when he saw me. I stopped and looked at him coldly. I'd said in my feelings everything I had to say, and didn't feel like trying to repeat any of it, especially in Italian. I pointed to my watch and said only, "*Piu di due ore da sola,*" ("More than two hours alone,") and looked at him searchingly.

A torrent of worried Italian poured out of him, little of which I understood. They'd reconnoitered ten miles outside of Warsaw, and everybody had panicked, he said, when they noticed I was missing. I wasn't ready to believe this, and I resumed pedaling. Antonio drove alongside me, still trying to explain through the open window. *Screw you all*, I thought, in a cold fury.

A few miles up the road, there they were, milling around in a big field beside the road. I was so angry I almost wished I hadn't found them, that I could have proceeded into Warsaw by myself. Who needed them? Not I.

Of course, it wasn't true. I did need them. They were my only people now, and I needed desperately to be part of the group; needed not to be isolated in the world; needed their goodwill, and loved many of them. I couldn't sort out my feelings; they were such a morass of relief, disappointment, anger, happiness to see them, embarrassment for my shortcomings which made them leave me, and raw rage.

Everyone gathered around to explain. There was Nino, looking as if he had nothing to do with it, as if I were some stranger in the group. I walked over to him and let him have it. "I thought we had a buddy system," I shouted. "I was off the back for more than two hours, and you knew and didn't even care!" My rage poured out. "Anything could have happened to me out there, but it would've been no skin off your nose! I've always kept track of where in the group you are riding, but all you ever think about is yourself!"

Confirming everything I'd said, he yelled back, "How dare you humiliate me like this in front of the men?"

I was so shocked at his total lack of concern for me and his complete self-absorption that I was struck speechless. I turned my anger to the group, waving my arms just like they did, "I'd just like to think that somebody here gives a damn about what happens to me!" For people who weren't supposed to understand any English, they understood every word. I wanted to say, "You'd never have let one of your own stay off the back for two hours," but I couldn't think of the Italian words. Some of their faces were taken aback; some angry; some mildly amused; and some worried and concerned, empathizing. Nino deliberately turned his back on me and began to justify himself to the group in Italian too rapid for me to understand.

Throwing up my hands in disgust, I walked away, thinking *I'm so sick of him I could scream*. I sat on a log. Maria Pia came over to give me a hug. I clung to her, biting my lip to keep from breaking down in the tears I was too proud to shed, but which were slipping out anyway. She gave me the last chocolate bar, and dabbed at my face with a hanky.

Luigi, Bruno, and other friends came over to explain that everyone had thought I was with another group and that they didn't keep such close track of me now that I was a better cyclist. They said that no one had meant to leave me and asked me to please believe that. I did. I knew it was the truth, knew the truth of my friends' caring. Probably.

Breathing deeply, I tried to calm down. Intense as I was, I had a long fuse and seldom in my life had I made such a scene. Now I just sat there on the log, elbows on my knees, looking at the ground in embarrassed misery, not knowing what to do next.

Everyone left, except Luigi. As I looked up, he extended his hands to help me up. Seeing that the others were diverted by a commotion over by one of the vans, he took my arm and led me behind a clump of trees and bushes. He held me tight, as if he were trying to put me back together. I surrendered to the moment, the feeling of his chest, the smell of him, his hands caressing my back, his breath. My feelings were in such a mess I didn't know what to do, except to try not to cry. With concern and something deeper in his eyes, he grasped my shoulders and shook me a little, bringing me back to myself. It was painful not to be able to talk to him. I stayed a little after he left, gathering what composure I could.

More people were gathered now by one of the vans, so I went over to see what was happening. Two men, who had stopped after seeing us from their passing car, were trying to question several cyclists, but they lacked a common language. Nino was summoned to see if they spoke English. They did. One man introduced himself as the president of the Polish Cycling Federation. He and his brother had been driving by chance in the opposite direction, and surprised, stopped to see who we were. It was unusual, they said, for a group as big as ours to cycle through Poland without their knowing about it. Who were we and where had we come from?

Nino explained, introducing Dottore and Antonio as the organizers of the group. (Dottore, after delivering Sergio to the airport, had arranged to be driven back so he could cycle into Warsaw with us.) Nino told the Polish visitors about our route, and conveyed Dottore's invitation to join us at the hotel tonight for our victory dinner. They gladly accepted and left, and we made ready to leave and cycle into Warsaw all together.

Dottore insisted I ride beside him. "*E non mi passa!*" ("And don't pass me!") he boomed, laughing and shaking a finger in my face.

"Okay, okay, *le promesso*," ("I promise,") I smiled, meaning it this time, loving this dear, autocratic man, and grateful that the tension I'd created had dissolved.

I decided to put the episode behind me, and to enjoy our triumphant procession—just as I'd visualized it!—through Warsaw. I looked around for Nino. Our differences had become too many and too great to patch up, like a car with too many dents; pretty soon you can't fix it anymore. Would we even be able to be friends, after this?

I turned my thoughts to the ride through Warsaw.

17

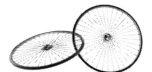

WARSAW

Arrivo!

The new Warsaw was a great surprise—especially after Prague, the medieval glory of which still stands, undamaged by centuries of European wars. Warsaw, in contrast, had been almost completely rebuilt since 1945, after having been bombed to smithereens during the war. The city's high-rises were large and modern, the boulevards wide. We couldn't look around much, due to our usual city dance through traffic, over tracks, trying not to run into each other or collide with cars or pedestrians in crosswalks, going through red lights trying to stay together.

Large, modern, lighted billboards for Marriott hotels and other Western companies, in English, vied for attention with skyscrapers and the huge, cell-block-like buildings that were products of the communist era. We pedaled along the big tree-lined boulevards, through the bustle of one of Eastern Europe's great metropolitan centers.

Warsaw, the seat of Poland's government, arts, and industry, has existed as a city since the twelfth century, wrenched back and forth between Russia, Germany, and an independent Poland. In 1794, half of its population was massacred and the city was burned by the Russians. In recent history alone, Warsaw had been made capital of the Polish Republic after the German occupation during World War I, only to fall again to the Germans in 1939. The siege of the Warsaw Jewish ghetto by the Nazis was one of the most horrifying tragedies of World War II. Nazi-occupied Warsaw fell to the Russians in 1945, and became part of the Soviet Union. By then there was little left of the bombed-out city, which the Poles, with the help of the Russians, undertook to rebuild. The Warsaw Pact—the Soviet version of NATO—was signed here in 1955, and only since the lifting of the Iron Curtain this year in 1990 could Warsaw once again proclaim itself the capital of a truly independent Poland.

Small wonder people on the streets here didn't smile and walked along with their hands thrust deep in their pockets. My Polish friend's words echoed within me: "*They could try to bomb us into oblivion, and we'd rise again, as we always have.*" He will forever to me be the voice of Poland.

As we approached the hotel, I scanned the pack for Old Luigi. I caught the twinkle of his eye, and for a split second we shared our triumph. I remembered his belly-shaking laugh and his grim determination as he pedaled with his bandaged head.

We made it. On the bicycle.

We rolled into the courtyard of our hotel to whoops, hollers, and cries of *"Complimenti!" "Complimenti!"* all around. The men slapped each other on the back and roared their approval to each other. Everybody hugged everybody else, and many of the men, even a few I didn't know, came over to offer their congratulations or to shake my hand.

I basked in the feeling of accomplishment. But more than a personal triumph, it was a validation of who I thought I was—no—who I was! It was one of those moments that etches itself into your memory; the afternoon sun warmed my shoulders and my matted hair as I stood leaning my elbow on the paw of a stone lion by the entrance to the hotel courtyard, my legs reveling in the blessed relief of being off the bicycle. I remember the rough, solid feel of the granite paw, grounding me in the moment. Filled with a deep elation that was a validation of having done what I'd believed I could do, I felt content and complete.

Sweat, Tears, and Joy

Spotting Gianni, I caught his eye and winked. He rolled his eyes and smiled, finally giving me the thumbs-up.

As I stood there basking in the success of our journey along with the rest of them, a man named Claudio, one of the ex-racer cyclists, came over. I'd never exchanged even so much as a word with him. Silently, he gave me the most gentle and tender embrace, tears in his eyes. Choking back my own emotions, I could only murmur, "*Grazie*, Claudio."

Old Luigi waved to catch my attention. Grinning broadly, he clasped his hands over his head, like a triumphant boxer. I laughed, returning the gesture.

Luigi came over. He took both my hands and looked into my eyes and said quietly, "*Complimenti, Lina. Ben fatto. Brava.*" ("Congratulations, Lina. Well done. Hooray for you.") He raised my hands to his lips, and his look reached all the way down my spine. He squeezed my hands for a long moment, turned, and left. I watched him walk away, wishing I could be walking beside him, this kindred soul. He stopped and looked back, feeling it.

I looked over at Nino. We hadn't spoken since the incident, by mutual consent. I walked over, not knowing what I'd say, but wanting to keep the mood of the occasion. "Hey, sparring partner," I said as lightly as I could manage, "we lived through another one. What do you say to at least a temporary truce?"

"Ah, Lina, Lina," he said with a great sad sigh, "what am I to do with you?" Not taking the bait, I no longer wondered what would become of Nino and me; I knew. I knew that he knew, too. But right now, it was time to celebrate.

"We made it, Nino, *complimenti*! C'mon, we earned this celebration today, just like everybody else—let's enjoy it!" Catching his arm, I pulled him over to Dottore, Luciana, Antonio, and the others amid sprays of wayward champagne, hugs, backslapping, laughter, and more giddy cries of congratulations.

By now our arrival commotion had dissolved into our bike packing commotion. Great rolls of bubble wrap appeared magically from the vans, amid frames, wheels, shouted instructions, tape sticking to the wrong stuff, people trying to find Luciana who dispensed the room keys, and more joyful whoops with the popping of corks, followed by geysers of champagne.

As we cleaned up and prepared for dinner, I luxuriated in donning my best female persona. After lingering in a long, hot bath, I put on the special aquamarine silk dress I'd brought for this occasion. It was simple and elegant, with slits on the sides and a deep V-neck. I loved the way it draped over my now-leaner body, clinging in all the right places. With my makeup pretty well camouflaging the lines of fatigue the wind had etched into my face, I thought I looked pretty damn good, considering.

We kept the conversation light as we dressed, avoiding mention of anything that might be controversial—and the list was growing. To say we were on different wavelengths was a gross understatement. It was a miracle we could understand each other when one of us said, "Pass the salt." "*Complimenti* to us, Nino, for getting here, though barely, without killing each other," I laughed, offering my hand. We shook hands, and to my great surprise, he pulled me to him and hugged me tight. Well, he'd remain as much of a mystery to me as I was to him. He offered his arm, and we went down to dinner.

Even before we entered the large dining room, I felt the excitement of our victory celebration spilling out the door in loud, happy Italian chatter. We sat at a big table with Dottore, Luciana, Bruno, Dino, and some of the others. Everyone was jubilant and in high spirits. Champagne flowed freely, and cheers rose from different parts of the room each time a cork popped.

Dino, who was very shy, never knew quite what to say to me, since he spoke no English. Usually he just conversed with Nino. But tonight, he turned to me and made a serious pronouncement, prodding Nino to translate. Nino told me that Dino wanted me to know that I had "learned to suffer like a man."

I stopped dead in my tracks, wine glass in mid-air, flooded with conflicting emotions. This was a most serious compliment. Deeply grateful, I accepted it in the manner it was given, even as I experienced an instant memory of the collective pain of woman—the pain of childbirth, the pain of losing husbands and sons in wars, the pain of survival in a world where men have the power and make the rules and there is little equity for women. I knew that woman's pain was not less, or less hard to bear, than man's. But this was a happy occasion. I raised my glass to Dino, and thanked him with all of my heart.

A waiter presented me with a bottle of special Italian Riccoto wine, indicating it was for our table from Luigi, who was seated across the room. As the waiter prepared to serve the wine, he slipped a card under my plate. It was from Luigi. On it was an address in Verona. He'd written, "Find me."

I turned, searching him out with my gaze. Looking at each other across the room and the chasm of our cultures, I nodded, and we raised our glasses in a private toast. I didn't know how, but I knew that somehow I'd see him again.

A glass was being tapped for a speech. I looked up to see Bruno walking toward our table, carrying a big bouquet of flowers wrapped in cellophane and ribbon. Everyone was quiet, and smiling. *Omygawd, they're for me!*

Bruno stopped in front of me, and motioned for me to stand. He placed the bouquet of pink gladiolus and ribbons in my arms. Clearing his throat, he spoke to me and to the room. Nino translated: "These flowers are a symbol of your successful completion of the journey, and of your courage. We want you to remember always: with sweat and tears, the flower always rejuvenates."

I was overcome at what a beautiful thing this was to say, and how much thought I knew they'd put into it. Prodding Nino for help with the words I didn't know, I thanked everyone for their friendship and their help, and for the opportunity to participate in this great adventure with them. Knowing the inadequacy of my words, I finally just put my hands over my heart and stretched out my arms to them in love and gratitude.

I sat down and looked around the room at these men I'd grown to love, their long legs stretched out askew, expressions of contentment on their tanned and weathered faces. I had a sudden urge to take each one of them in my arms and say, "Hey, wasn't it great?" My heart was full to overflowing. This was the stuff dreams are made of, and I would cherish this moment forever.

Epilogue

The Woman, the Price, the Cyclist

In the quiet of the night after the party, too excited to sleep, images of the journey drifted through my mind of this trip I shouldn't have been able to do, was not strong or well-trained enough to do. How had I been able to do this? That I did do it, what does that say about my—everyone's—real possibilities?

It had to do with what I've always called the decision point. There is a point on the continuum of your will at which the commitment to a decision is so deep and final that there are no other options except the completion of the goal. This totality of commitment merges with the successful completion of the goal—you have irrevocably linked your energy to it—so the goal becomes a fait accompli at the depth-point of the decision. Success is accomplished at that decision point, before the deed is done in the material world. The doing simply follows.

I propped myself up in bed on an elbow to admire the gladiolus. Elation flowed through my being and filled me with joy for having kept my promise to finish this journey on my bicycle. It was an incredible triumph for me personally, and also as a woman, to stake my place in the world and take it. Now I knew I could do it again, would do it again.

And I thought about the price. The vague cloud of discomfort, the one I knew so well, smudged the edges of my joy. It made me like a prickly thing, instead of a warm fuzzy woman who could move about in conventional society, following all the rules under the comforting umbrella of everyone's approval. Other paths I'd followed were in arenas claimed by men as their own. Most men don't like to cozy up to a woman like that. At times I'd been so terribly lonely that I wanted to go to my balcony and shout, "Hey, Wonderful Man out there somewhere, can't you see there's a really good woman here?"

But you have to be who you are. Even though my family raised me to be the independent woman I am, the pressure to conform to society's mold of "normal woman" was horrifyingly ubiquitous. I got it all day from my peers, business, TV, magazines, newspapers, men in my life, even my sons. Being who I am has always carried the uncomfortable feeling of going against the grain, swimming upstream. I wanted desperately to feel comfortable in the world. Sadly, the same qualities that have contributed to my discomfort are the very ones admired and encouraged in men: a strong will, assertiveness, initiative, an inquiring mind, speaking my truth.

So it was with a sense of poignancy that I claimed completing this trip as my personal victory. The other side of the coin was just what Nino had said; now, to some of them, I was just like one of the men.

But not merely, I thought. Luigi had respected the same qualities in me that had offended some of the others, and many of the men on the trip had accorded me the respect of an equal participant. Their willingness to accept me on whatever level I could participate and their help and good wishes had helped me to get here too; I wasn't pedaling by my effort alone. I stretched, filled with the joy of it. The price had not been too high.

Now I am a cyclist.

But what, exactly, I asked myself suddenly, is that? At once I knew with great clarity it wasn't about who was stronger, more skilled, or who won. I'd been a cyclist since I first laid foot to pedal when I was ten, on my first bicycle.

I'd been breathless with joy at the surprise of it, a gift from my mother and father, who stood proudly by. The memory is so clear: it was a shiny metallic royal blue, with white sidewalls on the black balloon tires. The medallion said "Monarch," and I was sure it was the best bicycle ever made. The sight of it instantly evoked pictures in my mind of country I'd pedal over, like an explorer. The world was mine!

Cycling is about a passion for life, manifested through a passion for a sport. It is qualities of mind and heart that make a cyclist; it is those qualities that allow a person to be a cyclist or to strive with heart's desire toward mastery in any sport—or any other endeavor at all.

The love and respect for what you're doing is the thing—to love and respect it enough to give not only all you have to give, the best you have to give, but also to surrender your limits, surrender to your possibilities, so you can give more, grow toward your best. It's on life's journey that you do this—again and again. It's the being there, on the road, that measures who is the cyclist. Like the Old Lady knew, it's showing up, with your heart.

Nino's and my lives diverged soon after we returned to California. He found a woman who probably didn't ask for second opinions, married her, and moved to Florida.

Although the gulf between Luigi's and my cultures, languages, and separate lives proved too great to bridge, the experiences we shared and the passion imbedded in them never diminished. It was the passion that changed the course of my life; I vowed never again to live my life without it. This decision continues to describe my life, drawing upon deep wells of courage that we all have, but that were only made conscious to me by this journey. It takes me now into uncharted territory paved with promise, as I stay on the road growing toward mastery in new talents and new ways of being.

I found and married "Wonderful Man," after many years of being single. This is indeed a new way of being, in which I am making some progress. My husband is English, and he says from time to time, "What am I to do with you, Lynne?"

I still ride my bike. I will ride my bike for as long as I can.

Acknowledgments

My heartfelt thanks to Nino, with whom I shared all these adventures and who made it all possible. I would like to thank Jim Schock, who was my original mentor and editor. I would also like to thank the late Lee Wagner for her editing help, the late Joan Allred, and my late mother-in-law, Inez Ashdown, both authors, who first made me believe I could and should be writing books.

My special thanks to Carolyn Grossman for her cover design and invaluable help with overall design of the book and the maps, and for her encouragement and friendship. I'm especially grateful to her for her belief in this project.

Many thanks to fellow author Michaele Lockhart for her help and advice, to Don Gilzinger for proofreading and editing, and to Maureen Wright for proofreading, and to all for their friendship. Thanks also to Richard McBain of Centric Photo in Tucson for his work on the route maps and photo finishing, and to Lori Leavitt at Wheatmark for her good work and her patience in producing this book.

I've called all of the Italians by their real names except Nino, which is his nickname. This is a true story, apart from liberties I've taken with the chronology of events.

Lynne Ashdown, Tucson, Arizona, June 2012

ABOUT THE AUTHOR

Lynne grew up roaming the hills of Oakland, California, pretending to be an explorer. Married and divorced young, she raised her two boys in Mill Valley, California. Fulfilling a lifelong dream, she became a singer-guitarist and played in venues around the San Francisco Bay Area.

Years later, her mother bribed her to stop singing in return for paying her way through college. She seized the opportunity and graduated from the University of California, Berkeley,

Photo by Britta Van Vranken

one year ahead of her oldest son. Her degree in (third world) Development Studies has served to deepen her vision of the world she writes about.

A native Californian, she also has lived in Hawaii, Libya, Italy, and England, and has traveled by bicycle over much of Europe and the western United States. Spurred on by an insatiable desire to know the truth of the world, in 2005 she walked over four hundred miles across Spain on the Santiago de Compostela Pilgrimage Trail. There are many truths, she learned, and her quest continues.

She became a writer through the back door in the context of work, before finally following her heart and publishing tales of her adventures in newspapers and magazines.

A longtime feng shui practitioner, she has also written *Twenty First Century Feng Shui for Your Home Office*, to be published soon. Also in the works is a tale of misadventures she experienced on the bike and with Italian culture while scouting cycle-touring routes in Italy for a guidebook. Writing is her joy.

She lives in Tucson, Arizona.

CPSIA information can be obtained at www.ICGtesting.com
Printed in the USA
BVOW070942210213

313746BV00001B/112/P